HEY AUNT HELEN !

Copyright © Kevin K 2022

All rights reserved.
No part of this publication may be reproduced, stored in or introduced into a database and retrieval system or transmitted in any form or any means (electronic, mechanical, photocopying, recording or otherwise) without the prior written permission of the author.

While every precaution has been taken in the preparation of this book. neither the author nor publisher shall have any liability to any person or entity with respect to any loss or damage caused, directly or indirectly by the information contained in this work.

contact: kevinkband@aol.com

ISBN: 978-0-6489302-2-8

Hey Aunt Helen !

Livin' Fast On The Road To CBGB

KEVIN K

This book is dedicated to the memory of:

Alvin K
Florence K
Alan K

The best cats – Joey, JJ and LuLu
I miss ya!

They are not lost who find the light of the sun, stars and God.

Alvin and Florence. The best rock 'n' roll parents

CONTENTS

Dedication — iv
Preface — ix
Foreword — xi

1. IN THE BEGINNING — 1

2. 1969 — 9

3. SNO-DAYS — 12

4. PENDLETONIANS — 14

5. SEPTIC TANK BLUES — 18

6. BERNICE AND THE FUNERAL HOME — 20

7. AUNT HELEN 1977 — 36

VI - CONTENTS

8	RECORDING OF BIG MONEY / REBECCA 7-INCH SINGLE	40
9	1972 CADILLAC	44
10	TOYS WILL DESTROY	46
11	1976 BORN AGAIN PUNK	53
12	AUNT HELEN LYRICS	66
13	MARK FREELAND	107
14	BAD BEHAVIOR	108
15	A-OK	110
16	RIDE ON WITH ALAN K	113
17	ST. MARKS RECORD STORE GOODBYE	132
18	BYE BYE MOM	135

19	JJ	140
20	A POEM FOR LULU	146
21	KEVIN K DAYS	153
22	WHICH MASK ARE YOU ?	156
23	DETROIT ROCK CITY 2022	158
24	ALVIN – MY ROCK 'N' ROLL DAD	163
25	KEVIN K DISCOGRAPHY (1978-2022)	167

PREFACE

I am happy to write this book. It has been an emotional struggle for me these last years. I didn't want to write a sad book. I waited until the tears receded before I began. It is important for me to write songs and stories because this is my therapy. If I ever do a third book it would be all the European stories I have, plus photos. There are many.

A crazy story. We had a show in Barcelona, Spain where they filmed a live porno movie before I played. Watching people have sex five feet from me in front of the stage was something the Aunt Helen band never experienced!

In this *Hey Aunt Helen!* book, you can read about some outstanding achievements I made in my early days. Without Alvin, Florence, Alan, the Aunt Helen Band, Tom Droz, Wayne Cozad, The Toys, Meat Clever, Doug Tyler and Peter Cain this book would never have happened.

The back cover photo is from France by Eric Brizaut. The Toys photos from Buffalo are by Jeanette Thalmann and D.J. Syracuse. The Lone Cowboys photos from New York City were by Donna Dietz. Every effort has been made to credit photographers for the use of tbeir photos, however this has not been possible in every instance. The use of your photo is appreciated and adds significantly to these stories. Thankyou. Note that many of the stories were written before Alvin passed away in 2020. Very special thanks to Colin Gray, Denis Gray and Kristine Isonhart.

I live my days laughing on the outside but crying on the inside.

Kevin, 2022

Photo: Judy Ridenour

FOREWORD

I met Kevin K through Bob Ballentine in 1980, or as he we called him back in the day, "Uncle Bobby". Bob was The Toys officially live recording engineer. He and I worked on the same college radio station together, WNCB. Bob told me I had to check out this really amazing Buffalo punk band called The Toys. So, he and I went to their gig at McVan's Capricorn Club in Buffalo. The Toys were regulars there.

The show was amazing, a lot of high-energy, on-stage antics, and some amazing vocals from all of them. Punk music at its best. I became an instant fan.

The night Bob introduced me to band members (Alan K, aka Rocky Starr, guitar/vocals; Kevin K, aka Kevin Rat, drums/vocals aka Kevin Rat; Joel Slazyk, aka Meat Cleaver, bass/vocals; Doug Tyler, aka Mick Tyler, guitar/vocals) and Mike Fechner, their sound guy and roadie. Everyone of them were very cool and personable.

A bit later, I saw Mike Fechner struggling to strike the PA, the guitar amps, and the drums after the show. Back then not a lot of clubs had their own sound system, and barely had lights, so bands had to bring their open PA system and equipment. So, I offer to give Mike a hand. When I got done helping to carry the PA speakers into Mike's van, I started striking the drum kit. I was almost finished with it when Kevin came over. He said I did an amazing job, and thanked me for helping out. He hated having to pack up the drums at the end of the night. Then, Kevin offered me a job of drum roadie, and I accepted.

That night started an amazing journey with everyone, from the days as The Toys to the New Toys. The band and I moved to New York City with a new bass player, Peter Cain, then later New Toys split up after Doug Tyler left. Nonetheless, Kevin and Alan went on to form the bands, Lone Cowboys, Road Vultures, and finally Kevin went solo. Over the years I was roadie, driver, tour manager, and friends to all of the different band's members. I also continued to work with Kevin and Alan along the way.

Of course, there was some tragedy along the way. First, we lost Alan K, then Peter Cain, and recently Mike Fechner. Nonetheless, I am still steadfast friends with those who remain, especially Kevin K. We were even roommates again in 1995, and was grateful to be able to produce a few recordings for him.

Kevin K has remained musically dedicated to those fledgling days of punk rock. The pioneer days of punk; the heyday of New York City punk. Kevin has played in almost every major rock music venue in NYC that are, unfortunately, lost now: Peppermint Lounge CBGBs, Hurrah's, Max's Kansas City, The Pyramid Club, Coney Island High, Brownie's, and so many more. The late 70s/early 80s music scene, the clubs, and the sub-culture influenced Kevin's music and performance style as much as did the New York Dolls, the

Ramones, The Stooges, Dead Boys, even Kiss and the Beatles. He became friends with Johnny Thunders, Sylvain Sylvain, Walter Lure, Cheetah Chrome and the members of Staten Island's Dirty Looks. Sadly, many of these great musicians and bands are now gone.

Nonetheless, Kevin K remains, carrying on the New York City punk sound, keeping it alive for the generations that missed those amazing days when NYC had had a real music scene. Kevin has brought his energetic music to Europe, Canada, the USA, and even Japan.

Yes, gone are those days, but Kevin remains. A true rock 'n' roller that has never given up and continues to record. Kevin K, I am proud to have been a part of those many years with you, and honored to be your friend still to this day.

Love you, brother!

Ted Sterns
NYC

The K Brothers were two of the nicest little miscreants I met in NYC. Funny, rockers to the bone, and a blast to hang with! Saw Kev on the last tour, and he hasn't changed a bit! Looking forward to reading this one !

Cheetah Chrome

Anyone who has been in this 'underground music' thing longer than ten years will see themselves in Kevin K's first book *How to Become a Successful Loser*. You will know him after reading his words. You may think he is pissing in the wind or tilting windmills. Knowing Kevin, he wouldn't argue with you. But check out his discography and the list of shows he has played over the years. It might cause you to ask yourself, *what have I done? Was I ever committed to the things I loved?* Only you know the answer. Me, I'm fond of Kevin K. A true lifer if ever there was one.

Pat Todd
Pat Todd and the Rankoutsiders

My friendship / musical companionship with Kevin K goes back almost 30 years. We've played all over the world together from Berlin to Tokyo to Hamtramck! Besides bonding on the obvious musical tastes and wonderfully warped sense of humor, we also share that same gritty blue collar ethic: he being from Buffalo and me from Detroit. We know what it means to really put the work in and get stuff done, even when it means doing it yourself. I'm sure Kevin will have a new album written and in the can by the time I've finished writing this! He is part of the chain of honest Rock and Rollers who will always follow their own path despite any trends or lack of (major) success.

Ricky Rat
Detroit

Kevin K is the Don Mattingly of rock 'n' roll. Despite a 14-year career with the New York Yankees, winners of the most World Series championships in baseball history, Mattingly, a six-time MLB Star first baseman and 1985 American League MVP, never got to use his sweet swing in the game's biggest showcase.

Most of Kevin K's 40-plus year career as a drummer, guitar slinger, singer and songwriter were spent in rock 'n' rolls major league epicenter, New York City. In the Lower East Side's CBGB league that boasted legendary All-Stars like Johnny Thunders, Joey Ramone and Cheetah Chrome, Kevin K churned out a huge library of sweet and powerful pop-punk songs, records and CD's. He earned the respect of top name stars and a legion of dedicated fans from his Buffalo, NY hometown to a series of small passionate rock 'n' roll towns across Eastern Europe, France, Germany and Japan.

Kevin K may never have gotten the chance to step up to the plate on a Madison Square Garden or Wembley Stadium stage, but those who watched him play as a member of Aunt Helen, New Toys, Lone Cowboys and Road Vultures with his late, great brother Alan, or through this millennium with a rotating army of Kevin K bandmates know a Hall of Famer when they see him.

Don Mattingly is so dedicated to the sport of baseball that he may never retire. He has become the manager of the National League's Miami Marlins, maintaining the glory of America's greatest game in the sunny climate of Florida. Across the state in Tampa-St. Petersburg, Kevin K manages the affairs of his amazing WWII veteran father, Alvin, a nonagenarian member of America's Greatest Generation.

And Kevin's music keeps on coming. It will always keep coming, no matter how many 'last time evers' he threatens. The songs, the recordings, the one-off American shows and the European tours. We wouldn't want it any other way.

Brian Dickman
Buffalo, NY

I met Kevin in 1995 as he was auditioning studios for his record *Party Down*. He said he looked at several places already. I gave him the studio tour and all the reasons why he should record the CD there (Tin Pan Alley Studios). In the end, he chose Tin Pan Alley, not because of me but because of…Pumpkin, the studio cat! His kind spirit, East Village New York attitude and great talent - are all the reasons we remain friends and collaborators to this day.

Patrick Klein
NYC Producer

Kevin K is a true 'lifer'. Back when we worked together, he was a rock star even standing behind the cash register. He eats, sleeps, breathes rock 'n' roll - REAL rock 'n' roll.

A disciple of my old friend Johnny Thunders, Kevin K has lived the life without getting into trouble. Thank God.

His songwriting is classic 3 or 4 chord punk with heart and brains. He has remained true to his school for decades and I am proud to be his friend.

Binky Philips
New York City

FOREWORD - XVII

I can't remember actually meeting Kevin K. He was just always around, he was always there. Not a part of a scene, more like a part of the landscape. It would have been the late 1980's or the early 1990's. It would have been the East Village, the Lower East Side when the general area was still unsoiled by hedge fund types and wine bars, before the sidewalks were cluttered with slaves to portable cellular technology. It was probably at the counter of Sounds or Venus on St. Marks Place. It was not a conversation about grunge or hip-hop or last week's underground techno releases. Or maybe it was 11:15 PM at The Horseshoe Bar. Kevin was always around, always there long before we knew each other.

By the summer of 1998 my band Sour Jazz was up and running and gigging and recording. Our guitar slinger, the World-Famous Mr. Ratboy already shared a history with Kevin through having played guitar on some of Kevin's earlier studio albums. Sour Jazz may have shared a bill or bills with Kevin or maybe Rat convinced Kevin to come to one of our gigs but it was through Rat's connection with Kevin that three quarters of Sour Jazz were invited to Tin Pan Alley in 1999 to play the sessions for what would become the *Bloodied Up* album by Freddy Lynxx & the Corner Gang. Alongside Kevin was Freddy, Elda Stiletto (RIP), as well as Wild Bill Thompson (RIP) and Philippe Marcade out of The Senders. In other words, a super group not likely to trouble the Billboard chart compilers.

Unless Kevin's been sneaking around behind my back, I have been his bass player for every NYC gig he has played ever since that Tin Pan Alley session. A working relationship that has now outlived the vast majority of venues that we have played together over the years. In a world overly full of bands who think of everything except the song, Kevin has always put the song first. Anything else that comes along for the ride, attitude, riffs, swagger and whatever else ride in the back seat, complementing the song through the shade and color. And it's this skill and discipline as a songwriter along with his resolute dedication and genuine enthusiasm, that always makes gigging with him a hell of a lot of fun. His songs are sonic comfort food. But scratch beneath the sheen of Thunders and the Stones and you'll not only hear bits of Howlin' Wolf, Jimmy Reed and Lightnin' Hopkins but also echoes straight from the corridors of the Brill Building.

As Pope XIV remarked in 1773, the man knows his shit. For now though, forget everything I have written above. My favorite Kevin shaped memories are the hours of conversation in rehearsal rooms, bars and venues, taxis, sidewalks, bodegas and late-night street corners.

Sometimes enlightening, sometimes entertaining, always engaging. Kevin has spent a lifetime collecting experiences and filling observations, not all light, not all dark but all worth retelling. This book should do the job of putting you on the stool next to his as he tells his tales.

Mark Rubenstein
Sour Jazz
Kevin K and the Bowery Kats

Even though he will firmly deny it, I'm convinced the Twister Sister song *You Can't Stop Rock 'n' Roll* was written about Kevin K. If it wasn't it should have been. Starting his career in Buffalo, Kevin eventually made his way to stage right as a guitarist in NYC and finally ended up where he truly belongs, center stage, singing in every rock club cool enough to book him. Upon reaching his rightful position, the music started pouring out of him and never stopped. After digesting his impeccable musical influences, Kevin quickly transcended them and created his very own styles rooted in his honest and unshakeable faith in the music he grew up with. I must admit I lost count of how many albums he has put out, but I do know that all of them are loaded with the kind of songs that remind me of why I fell in love with rock 'n' roll in the first place.

It hasn't always been a smooth ride, but when knocked down by adversity, Kevin always got back on his feet and soldiered on with abandon, a guitar slinger Energizer Bunny that just keeps going and going.

Such a lifestyle produces countless unique anecdotes and Kevin's first book *How to Become a Successful Loser* simply could not contain them all. Don't worry, he wrote a second book and you're holding it right now.

Mr. Ratboy - Tokyo, Japan
Motorcycle Boy, Pillbox
Sour Jazz, The Golden Rat

I first met Kevin...hmmmm.. I don't really know when. It kind of feels like he has always been around. He is that kind of guy that I like, I appreciate, I respect. I remember both The Toys and the New Toys. In those days I was promoting quite a bit around Buffalo, Cleveland, Pittsburgh and Erie. I am sure I saw them a few times, hell I even think we played on some of the same gigs. Truth be told that was a lot of brain cells ago. I can't tell you for sure if those memories are real or not? Hmmmm.

By the mid/late 80's, I was based full time promoting and managing in New York City. At that time, I was managing Sylvain Sylvain and also Jerry Nolan & the Ugly Americans. It was also the time that Kevin, now with the Lone Cowboys, seriously appeared on my radar. This I am very sure about. On through the Road Vultures and the Kevin K Band, he has remained on my radar ever since as a performer, songwriter, author and friend.

You already know that Kevin is a top-notch player at drums and guitar. He is a consummate songwriter and exciting performer and a captivating author. His words, his style, his performance in the medium he chooses is done in a way as to draw the listener, viewer, reader into the world, the life of Kevin K. He draws you in with a familiarity. He makes you feel like you are side by side with him. Through the ups and downs, the joys, the pains, the sorrows and tragic loss, and the will to overcome.

His journey is our journey, the journey of those who love rock 'n' roll, love life, possessing the unwavering desire to do it our way. Not to fear losing, not struggle and to never look back with sadness, but to always move forward with hope.

His performance is wonderfully, perfectly imperfect, in the way that it always comes from the gut, the feeling, the heart of that moment in time. Not from perfection of the record but from the passion to make all he does sound and feel relevant and new, like the creation of each note, work, hook, manifested itself at that very moment in time. That's the Kevin K I know. The Kevin K that has always been around. The Kevin K that proves to me why I love rock 'n' roll.

Kipp Elbaum
New York City Promoter

I was born in 1974, too late to experience what I consider the best of rock 'n' roll. By the time I was twenty most of my favorites were dead. Thunders, Stiv, Rob Tyner, even GG Allin. There were some remnants, but they all evolved into something different. I thought I had missed everything. Then in 1995, I found the Road Vultures *Ride*. I now had an immediate tie to the past through Kevin K. Kevin along with a very few others is the last of not only a dying breed but a breed that will never be replaced. These times aren't capable of producing this brand of rock 'n' roller. Let's hang onto him as long as we can.

Duane Rollick
Shitcan Dirtbag, Murder Junkies
Kevin K and the Krazy Kats

I first met Kevin while working at St. Marks Sounds record store in the East Village in 1984. He proceeded to enlighten me constantly by playing Iggy Pop, the New York Dolls and Johnny Thunders.

Kevin also had great bands at the time. The Lone Cowboys and the Road Vultures, who brought me into the underground world of CBGB on a regular basis. In that environment, Kevin then with brother Alan K (RIP) played hook-laden original songs as well as choice covers by the Dolls, MC5 and the like. Hot music in sweaty clubs. Since then, Kevin and his music have been a constant in my life, from the days we worked together in the store, to the era of Road Vultures and Kevin K Band in CBGB and on Circumstantial Records.

From shows in Buffalo to Tokyo, hanging with Kevin has been one wild, exhilarating ride packed with great music and total character. Kevin K. Curator of Rock. What you are about to read is a guidebook to rock 'n' roll. FIRE IT UP!

Elmer Germack
Circumstantial Records

Discovering Kevin K rock 'n' roll more than 25 years ago now was akin to finding the Lost Dutchman's Gold Mine. I hit the jackpot! Here was a guy writing catchy power-pop better than Westerberg and Chilton combined. Heavy on the melody, sweet harmonies, killer guitar riffs and sing-along choruses. I am yet to find another musician who can write guitar heavy, infectious pop songs as consistently well as Kevin K. Kevin's commitment to his art is perilously total, nestled alongside an indifference to the ever-problematic question of commercial success in the music world. There are those who believe that success is a meritocracy, yet I don't buy that. For the most part, creative success has little to do with talent or hard work. Lots of people are talented and hard-working. Yet you also need luck - and connections. So, you should always remember that success is not a measure of worth. Once you stop believing in meritocracy, solidarity gets a lot easier. There are Kevin K converts, people like you and me - enlightened, united rock fans all over the globe, who recognise that in the end — it's the music that matters - and it's the music that endures.

His song writing prowess has ripened over the years too. The Johnny Thunders influence is as present as ever, yet Kevin is attuned to America's World War II history as much as he is NYC 70's punk. In recent years he has presented the listener with evocative themes that range from the D-Day Landings to Cold War Europe and the Manhattan Project. As a songwriter who has now penned literally hundreds of distinctly melodic songs - he confirmed long ago that he's no one-trick pony.

In an age when music is manufactured, contrived, disposable and lacking in any authenticity - you can always depend on Kevin K. The guy has more rock 'n' roll credential than anyone you care to name. He is #1. The music matters still. It always will.

Colin Gray
Vicious Kitten Records
Australian Rock Show Podcast

| 1 |

IN THE BEGINNING

I decided to name my second book *Hey Aunt Helen!* This was the name of our first real band. Many stories are from my childhood. It shows how all this weird, early life shaped my later thinking and writing life.

My first book *How to Become a Successful Loser* was a generalization of my entire existence. Now with this second book, I'm just writing about a small period. The beginning of something horrible! We as the Kalicki family should have had a reality TV show. It would have been just as interesting as *The Osbournes*.

Alvin and Florence never really had hard rules for Alan and me. We were taught to respect other people. If we didn't, Alvin would hit us with a pair of wet underwear or a belt. It was a military way of thinking. I use this now on Alvin in his late life. Except I don't hit him with wet underwear.

My first idea for the book was just all photos and

advertisements. I have so many it seemed like a cool idea. Then I could throw everything in the dumpster. That's my life's goal. Get rid of a lot of the past information. I started remembering so many stories of life in Pendleton. Maybe you all have these types of stories in your life also? The last few years, 2015-2017 have been the worst for me. The deaths of my mother and best cat JJ just seemed impossible to get through. I almost cracked up.

To become a regular 'Joe' and pay bills, banking, cooking, cleaning, making sure the 93-year-old man washes and eats and takes his Docusate, Simvastatin, Finasteride, Donepezil and Tamsulosin. This was a complete change for me. I also order all his VA (Veterans of the U.S. Armed Forces) medicines and book his appointments. Alvin's doctor told me I am a hero because of all the help I am to Alvin. He says I am doing an excellent job. So that makes me feel good. I am keeping history alive for as long as I can.

Alvin was in WWII. Drafted at 18 in 1943. Sent to Camp Gordon Johnston, Florida. This is where they taught him jungle warfare. He was there for almost one year. Then shipped to the Philippines with General MacArthur. The heat and the humidity were very bad. Many soldiers came down with malaria in this Pacific theater. Alvin did three amphibious landings on the Higgins Boat (Landing Craft Vehicle Personnel or LCVP), which are those little boats that are filled with thirty men. It goes right onto the beach, big front gate opens, and you run like hell with your gun over your head. It is amazing he survived this. He was in the seventh wave at Luzon Province, Lingayen Gulf. They followed the infantry as it advanced all the way to Manila.

He was a Litter Bearer, which is a soldier that helps with wounded men. Lifting patients onto stretchers and carrying them to aid stations. He was also an engineering specialist. That means he knew how to build bombs. The atomic bombs were dropped on Hiroshima, Japan on August 6, 1945 and then on Nagasaki, Japan on August 9, 1945 while Alvin was in Manila.

He was then sent to Nagasaki as part of the first occupation troops. His company took over a former Japanese Camp at Omura near Ishahaya on Kyushu, the third largest island of Japan's five main islands. Alvin drove through the streets of Nagasaki and Hiroshima in an open truck surveying the destruction and looking for survivors.

In Pendleton, I remember Alvin was always fooling around with chemicals and gas in the shed. I don't think he was making weapons. Maybe he was making a new fuel for our barbecue. Alvin remembers some stories about the war. He told me many times they would be attacked by Japanese planes flying low over the beach. They called this strafing. Alvin would be laying on his back shooting his gun up at the planes. He said one plane crashed and burned, the pilot ejected but landed right next to the plane that was on fire. They covered the body in a captured Japanese flag.

After his basic training, and prior to boarding his ship from San Francisco to the Philippines, Alvin's Commander told him to write a letter to his mother telling her goodbye, because if he came home, it would be in a box. It blows my mind for him to have that thought on a ship for one month getting to the Philippines. How do you deal with that?

There were snipers in the trees, so you never knew when

you could get shot. It is very difficult when you are fighting an enemy that didn't care if they lived or died. Plus, don't forget that the Japanese and the German soldiers were older and experienced at war. The American soldiers were just young kids of eighteen to twenty, but still won the war. These are heroes. Alvin knew a guy in his platoon that would approach the dead Japanese soldiers, open their mouths and dig out their gold fillings with his bayonet. He came home with a small bag of gold. That is hardcore. Alvin also had to do a thing called 'stick-um', which meant if he saw a dead Japanese soldier he had to 'stick-um' with his bayonet to make sure they were dead. This was the brutality of WW II.

When Alvin was sent to Japan with the first occupation troops, he said the Japanese people were fantastic, friendly and nice to him. I can't find them now, but I remember seeing some photos of Alvin with the geisha girls.

We had a compensation claim with the VA because Alvin came down with many cancers, attributed to being exposed to radiation. No gloves. No masks. Alvin was in the 'hottest' spot in the hypocenter in the downwind fallout area near the Nishiyama Reservoir. This Reservoir was 3 km from the hypocenter of the Nagasaki atomic bomb. After a six year wait, the decision was made...DENIED. The government just basically said a human could not have lived for another seventy years after being exposed to radiation. I told the Army judge, 'Maybe Alvin is like Keith Richards, there are just some people who can survive anything.' He didn't buy it. My mother, Florence was a rivet girl in Buffalo. She worked putting rivets into P59 Fighter planes. As a kid, my mother made 'Four Dicks of Death', that's beef links with beans, and 'Shit on a Shingle', that's gravy on toast. Military meals. Good and simple. Made me strong like a bull.

So, there are moments of disarray every day. I told Alvin if he ever starts wearing an adult diaper, it's over. I'm not getting into that business. I can't believe I escaped the 'real life' for twenty years. It's not for me at all.

I helped Alvin sell two houses, we made money, plus two mortgages, moving companies, plane flights for the cats to Buffalo and back to Tampa. Also, taking care of Florence's death with all the stupid paperwork.

After Florence died, Alvin and I moved to Buffalo for eight months. We did what Florence wanted. She wanted to finish her life back in Buffalo. Sad, she didn't make it. It was nice. The smell of the woods brought me right back in time. I had a full basement in which I set up my 'toys' - drums and amps. I recorded sixty songs. I felt like it was 1981 again when Alan and I would record some songs and go outside in the backyard and smoke a cigar and listen to them. Oh, and I never changed the drumheads. They were from 1986 and still sound good. Jerry Nolan was the last person to play them.

I also got to see Dave Constantino play live a few times. He was the guitarist from Talas. Meat Cleaver and I went to see him play in Niagara Falls. We were late, so Dave was already playing when we arrived. To hear his voice over the PA system outside the bar reminded me of when we would listen to Talas outside a bar in Lockport in 1976.

Alvin got a VA loan for relocation back to Florida. We moved back. I found a cool house. This was 2015. I painted it, planted 140 plants and trees, did a really nice job. I watched many episodes of *This Old House*, a program about making an old house look new again.

So then, Irma, the hurricane comes through. It was dangerous. This was not going to be a dainty wind event. The police came down the street on loudspeaker telling everyone to get out and stay at shelters. We decided to stay in the house with the shutters down. Of course, Alvin slept through the whole storm. He was constipated. I stayed in the living room with my portable CD player. I had Tom Petty and Iggy Pop CD's. I drank half a pint of whiskey and was completely drunk with LuLu and JJ when the hurricane was coming down our street. The entire house shook, with stuff hitting the windows and front door. The power went out at 11:00 PM and I'm in the dark with the cats and music playing loud. I heard a huge explosion in the backyard. I could not get out of the house to see what happened. My first thought was that a small plane has crashed in the backyard, or maybe a rocket from Kim Jong-un.

By 5:00 AM it was over. When I went outside there was a fifty-foot tree that had fallen ten feet from our screen room. If it had of hit the house, it would have gone right through. Fifteen of my favorite trees that I had planted were pulled right out of the ground. Also, there are no police or help until the storm is over, so you are on your own when you decide to stay. We could have died. Afterwards, there was no power for three days. This is when we decided to sell the house. Too many things to worry about.

We didn't have much insurance on the house, too

expensive. Nice place, but right in the flood zone. I read a story in the newspaper about the condition of the shelter in a high school that we were supposed to be at. It was disgusting. They found human poop and pee everywhere. Used toilet paper in school desk drawers, toilets overflowing, no water or food. And once you check in, you can't leave until they let you. So many people were there for three days. Bullshit. Alvin would never go for that.

We flipped the house (means bought and resold) and made a lot of money. I also had to sell it because the backyard was my cat JJ's. He loved that yard and was always outside with me every day. JJ would catch lizards and eat them. After he died, I could not go back there anymore. When we listed the house, it sold in two weeks.

I stopped touring for the next two years and just played in Florida only. Probably the smartest thing I have ever done in my life. That is something I haven't done in the last fifteen years. It was also the most time I have spent with my father since I was a little kid. He does odd things now, especially with the cats. I found the litter box filled with bird seed, not cat litter. He said, 'What's the difference?' He woke me up at 4:00 AM to tell me he was going to feed the cats. I said, 'No, I will feed them when I get up.' At 9:00 AM I got up and went into the kitchen to feed the cats. I found the cat dishes filled with those small batteries that fit in Alvin's hearing aid. I guess they do look like dry cat food.

It's amazing how much the human spirit can stand. When you lose complete control of a situation that has no solution it drives a person almost insane. Alvin helped me with my first ten years of life, so I must help him with his last ten years of life.

Semper Fi.

| 2 |

1969

1969 was the first moon walk. We watched it on our black and white TV set with a coat hanger on top as an antenna. Reception was good.

After seeing this guy walking on the moon and hitting a golf ball, I didn't think it was real. The next day at school, Starpoint Central, the Principal Mr. Fricano made a big speech to our class. This was right after we said the Pledge of Allegiance to the Flag and then we had our morning air raid drill where we would cover our heads under our desks for two minutes. The preparation for the Cold War. I enjoyed this. The Pledge to the Flag was great. I felt like I was in the Army.

Anyhow, after listening to Fricano's speech about the great American moment we had just seen, I told our teacher and other kids it was fake. They filmed everything in the desert. Well, I was in BIG trouble. They sent me home, called my parents. I was suspended for three days. OK with me, I would spend my days on our hockey rink practicing.

My parents didn't make a big deal about what I said. I think they thought it was fake too.

Alan and I used to get our hair cut by Coletti, the barber. Downtown Lockport. We both had brush cuts almost like skinheads. My mother would always be worried watching Coletti cut our hair. On one of his hands, his little finger had a really long nail. I don't know why he had this. Maybe for good nose picking. Don't think he was snorting coke off that nail, but Florence thought he was going to poke my eye out with that thing. Haircuts were one dollar. We always watched Irv Weinstein on WKBW-TV for our news. He was a smart guy. I don't remember him ever having his own opinion about the stories he read, unlike today where everything is covered in shit. I hate it. I can't tell what's real or fake.

The weather guy Tom Jolls did the weather report outside, even when it would be ten degrees below zero and snowing. Tom also hosted *The Commander Tom Show*, our favorite.

There was a cool TV show we used to watch from Toronto, *The All-Night Show* with Chuck the Security Guard. He was a security guy who would come into the studio at night and play videos.

This was 1979. In fact, I found episodes on YouTube. Crazy to see that again. It seems TV played a large role in my childhood. We were never bored. Always searching for something new. Alan and I waited until we were in our late twenties before using drugs. Everything we did was natural.

Once in a while a few Tylenols with a can of Coke. Just to take the edge off the day.

If I ever told my father I was depressed, he would tell me to get over it and get off my ass and walk two miles to Horan's grocery store on Main Road and buy some Mountain Dew and potato chips. We would eat one full pound can of chips in a day. Sometimes we would buy a giant block of cheddar cheese because we could get many different cheeses from Canada. By late afternoon, the whole block of cheese and the one pound can of chips would be gone.

Monty Python was important to us. Lots of funny stuff. Intelligent comedy. I had many private fantasies. I'm glad we didn't have Facebook or the internet. Pendleton was the real world. We as Aunt Helen had a tactile sense. All this information was used in our writings.

| 3 |

SNO-DAYS

So many winters in Pendleton were brutal cold and snow. We had five acres of land in the back. Great for football, baseball and dirt bike racing.

Our next-door neighbor Leonard, Alan and I once caught a snake. We decided to sacrifice it. We put it in a large can, poured gas on it and fired it up! The fire got completely out of control and set the entire backyard on fire. Flames were ten feet high. My father called the Wendelville Fire Department. The truck arrived and two of the fire fighters were smoking cigarettes. They said there was nothing they could do but control the burn. We burned down the entire five acres of field and trees, and almost two houses. The Lockport Police arrived and said they could arrest us for careless fire burn. I think it was to scare us. It didn't.

This was the same field where I sat and looked at my first Playboy Magazine. Hot Lips from the TV show *M*A*S*H* was on the front cover.

Our house was at least 500 feet from Main Road. In the winter, the driveway would be filled with tons of snow. So Alvin decided to build a snowplow. He built it from plywood. It looked like the front of a snowplow truck. Alan and I would be in front like two horses and pulled it up and down the driveway. I think this is how I first developed back problems. Alvin thought it was a waste of money to pay someone to plow because after one hour, the driveway was covered again. With his 'Polish Plow', we could use it all the time.

It would be five degrees in the Aunt Helen garage and rehearsal room. We had a wood burning stove to warm it up. Sometimes it wouldn't let the smoke out, and the garage would be filled with smoke while we rehearsed. We felt like KISS, only we used real smoke.

Our days would be filled with morning snow plowing and then hockey practice in the front yard rink pretending I was Billy Knibbs. He was a player with the Buffalo Bisons Hockey Club. Number 12. Then at night, Aunt Helen rehearsal where I would pretend I was Peter Criss. Good Times.

| 4 |

PENDLETONIANS

Alan and I found a small hill way back in the woods behind our house. We took small shovels and started digging and we found many very old medicine bottles from the 1950's. Some were blue colored glass and some were green. I think there was a store built there at one time and this was the garbage dump. My parents were selling some antiques inside the Aunt Helen practice room (the garage). We sold some of the antiques for a lot of money. I wrote lyrics from this adventure in my song *My Little Backyard*.

We had a small football field behind the house. Alan and I cut down some trees, built goal posts and painted them white. I would pretend I was Bruce Alford. Buffalo Bills kicker in the 1960's.

During the night, someone knocked them down. This happened a few times. So, we got mad. We took barbed wire that we bought from Boblocks hardware store and stretched it ten feet across and tied it to low trees. When it became dark, whoever it was would trip and fall and get stabbed in the heart and die. Alvin helped us. I think it reminded him of the war with all the Japanese booby traps. No one ever got killed and we found out later who it was. Some friends from down the street fooling around.

On the corner of Main Road and Mapleton Road, there is a big red barn. It is still there. I saw it when I visited Pendleton about four years ago.

Well, behind that barn, when I was eight years old, I dropped my pants, and the little girl who lived in the house in front, also about eight years old, dropped her dress. We showed each other our private parts. No big deal. I didn't even know what I was seeing. I didn't care. Funny, now that's all I care about.

Alvin made us cut the entire five acres of grass a few times with one push lawnmower. It took three days to cut. Harsh payment maybe for dropping my pants. He never said anything.

In the summer, I remember finding hockey pucks in the woods after the snow had melted. I still think about going into those woods and looking for the pucks I shot over the wooden boards that Alvin constructed. That would be strange to find a puck I had put there in 1968.

There was no such thing as a hockey stick with a curved blade back in 1968. We would take our sticks, pour hot water on them, shove them under the door and then pull them up to bend them. We tied them up overnight. Next day it would be completely bent. In practice before a game at Kenan Center, I was shooting slap shots that sent the puck ten feet in the air, almost hitting a few kids in the face. Very dangerous.

I was like a miniature Bobby Hull. The coach took the stick away and sent me to the bench.

Alan had a great idea. He took his football helmet, and had my father cut it with a band saw so it was still a football helmet, but with the face guard and ear protection cut off. It was super cool looking.

When Buffalo Sabres player Steve Atkinson came to the Kenan Center for an autograph session, he saw Alan's helmet and asked him, 'Where did you get that?' Alan said, 'My Polish father cut up my football helmet with his band saw.' Wouldn't you know it, a couple months later we see a photo in *The Courier Express* newspaper and Steve Atkinson is wearing a hockey helmet made from a football helmet. No thanks and no autograph.

We had a dog named Chugger who was on a twenty-foot leash right in front of the garage. This dog was so crazy strong he would drag his doghouse fifty feet to our back door when wanting to eat. He broke off the leash, ran to the road and was hit and killed by a pickup truck.

Next to the garage we had a storage shed which had all kinds of Alvin's chemicals and tools. We had a chicken named Heather who would lay brown eggs in there. My mother's cat, Pansy, would sometimes sit on the eggs to keep them warm while Heather was in the yard eating and talking with the other chickens we had. We were like a family from the TV show *Hee Haw*.

Since the dog was gone, Alvin decided that we needed a light above the garage for protection. He installed a big lamp in front of the garage. So about one week later, I'm in the bathtub and I reach to turn on more hot water. Bing! I get a small shock like static electricity. Weird. This went on for about two weeks. We all just thought it was nothing.

Then one time, I have the bathtub filled and I had a radio next to the tub. I would listen to Rick Jeanneret broadcast the Buffalo Bison's hockey games from The Aud. While I am touching the radio, my other hand is on the fixture for hot water. Wow! I get shocked and almost knocked out of the bathtub. Something is really wrong.

We have an electrician come over who inspects Alvin's wiring job on the lamp above the garage. He can't believe there is no ground wire and it's on the same line as the lights in the bathroom. Pure electricity was going into the wall and electrifying the bathroom fixtures. We could have been electrocuted. I could have been killed by the Aunt Helen light. That would have been bad. Still Alvin didn't believe it. Said it was my imagination. When my mother found out, she said to Alvin, 'You big, dumb Polock!'

| 5 |

SEPTIC TANK BLUES

Our Pendleton house had our own well for water. It was at the side of the house. The water was OK, but kind of odd tasting. Washing clothes was OK, but when we took baths, afterwards, my skin became tough as leather. My face started to look like a baseball catcher's mitt. Wrinkly and dry from hard water.

Ferguson Oil Company filled our tank behind the house. Once in the middle of winter we ran out of oil. A large empty cistern. The pipes were frozen. So, Alvin took a blow torch out and used it on the pipes to unfreeze them. I thought everything would catch on fire. Would have been a warm bonfire.

Ferguson could not get to our house for three days because of the snow. It was like living in Alaska. In the middle of the winter a very bad smell was coming from our backyard. Like dead animals. Just could not figure it out. We had to circumnavigate. Finally, the snow started to disappear. Yup, there it is, the entire backyard is covered in poop. Our septic tank was overflowing so it filled the backyard with real fresh poop. It looked like Somalia in the summertime.

We had to hire a company to come over and empty the septic tank and vacuum up all our dinners. Disgusting.

Alan and I once tried to make wine. We had two large jars. Filled them up with grapes and water and sugar. We learned from a TV show called *The Galloping Gourmet*. My mother used to watch it at 4:00 PM every day. We buried the jars in the yard and waited about six months. Dug them up, opened the jars. There it is, Kalicki wine. Tasted like kerosene.

We also tried to smoke. Alan took the comic section from the newspaper. We rolled it up really tight into small cigarettes and smoked it. I smoked the *Peanuts* comic. No good. We also built a super cool tree house. Way up high I could watch the neighbor's mother sunbathing. That was good fun. I could also throw rocks at the mailman. We were very impetuous.

I think growing up in the city, kids get to see and learn about real life. Growing up in the woods for Alan and me, we really had to use our imagination about the outside world. Places like CBGB, New York City, musicians like Johnny Thunders, Dead Boys and the Ramones turned out to be just like we envisioned them.

I can still remember our phone number from forty-five years ago. 716-434-7029.

| 6 |

BERNICE AND THE FUNERAL HOME

My father's mother Bernice came right from Poland to Ellis Island in the 1920's. They first moved to Brooklyn, then Batavia and finally Buffalo. She was a nice grandmother.

Alvin told me his father pulled out one of his sister's teeth with pliers when it got infected. Didn't believe in spending money to visit a dentist.

Every Christmas was a big get together of the Kalicki family at Bernice's apartment on Hertle Ave. At least thirty people would be there. My father's sisters Millie and Clarice would be smoking and getting drunk on whiskey. My Uncle John had a cool hardware store, also on Hertle Avenue, where Alvin bought all the supplies to build the house in Pendleton. Uncle Johnny let Alan and I play with his Buffalo Bills football that he had caught in the end zone at a game at

War Memorial Stadium in the 1960's. He had season tickets with my Uncle Carmen.

Homemade Polish food was always served. My favorites were Paczki (Polish doughnuts) and Chruscki, which I can now buy in St. Petersburg. This fun time celebration went on from 1965-85. Bernice died in 1988. That's when it all ended. Never saw the family again. I still remember Alvin calling me at Sounds record store in NYC to tell me.

Every Sunday, after we went to Good Shepherd Church in Pendleton for service, we would visit both Grandmas. At church there was a family that we would always get stuck sitting next to. The father we named, 'The Fourth Grader'. We had nicknames for everyone. It was our own special code. Anyway, the father acted like a kid, and he had four kids with him. The kids were crying, running up and down the church aisles, the priest yelling at them many times to be quiet.

I was always creeped out when going to Confession. You kneel down in a little booth and the priest listens through a little window. You really can't see him. My sins were always the same, swearing and pissing in the backyard. Once Alan and I covered the girl next door's bike in dog shit. We rubbed it everywhere. The seat, handlebars and basket. She was a bitch to us. That was a sin. I had to say many Hail Mary's after that.

We would drive in Alvin's yellow Gremlin to visit Bernice on Hertle Avenue in Buffalo. She had a small one-bedroom apartment. If there was a Buffalo Bills football game on, we would go over to the funeral home that she worked at answering phones. They had a nice big color TV. I remember so many games with O.J. Simpson, Jack Kemp and Elbert 'Butter Fingers' Dubenion. We called him that because he could never catch a pass.

We would watch the games on TV, but in the next room there would be a dead body lying in an open coffin. It was prepared for visitation. Even when we would go to Catholic funerals, we would see the dead body and then in the next room there would be a large table with lots of meats, cheese, bread, etc. How can anyone eat after viewing a dead body? I still can't figure that one out.

When Alvin came home after the war, he brought back many items, including a Japanese rifle which today would probably sell for $2,000. So, a few weeks after being back home at Bernice's, Alvin can't find the rifle. He asked his mother, 'Where is the Japanese rifle?' She tells him she didn't want any memories of the war in her house. Bernice has taken the rifle and thrown it over Niagara Falls!

I still have the two knives Alvin wore on his Army belt between 1943 and 1946, and many patches from his service in the Philippines.

My mother's family was the Loszkas. Mary (her mother), Eddie (Florence's brother) and Aunt Helen lived in a small apartment on Jermain Street in a city named Black Rock in Buffalo. Hardcore Polish section. Her mother and Aunt Helen would always speak in Polish when they were talking about me. I think they were saying that I had a weird head and was going to grow up a loser.

Uncle Eddie was a hardcore beer drinker. We would visit them early Sunday mornings and Eddie would be on his second beer. Alan and I couldn't stop laughing sometimes because Eddie would sit at the big steel kitchen table in a low chair so all you could see was just his head and the beer bottle. It was unbelievable to see. I think he would get mad at us. Kind of a sad life for the Loszkas.

Grandma Mary was excessively taciturn, and never threw out the newspapers. In the living room there would be newspapers that were five years old. She was almost dulled by life. She spoke about everything the same.

Aunt Helen believed the President lived in a castle on a hill. When my parents moved to Lakeland, Florida for six months (Alvin took a job to make a lot of money), Helen could not understand why my parents couldn't come by and visit since Florida was only fifteen minutes from Buffalo. Aunt Helen was a decent person Dziekuja - Stadagotcha. This means thankyou - and brown underwear.

Their apartment was always cold, dark and creepy. Velvet paintings of Jesus on the Cross everywhere. Also, on the kitchen table there was always butter shaped as a lamb. I guess it was a Catholic thing. Oh, and Eddie's Pabst Blue Ribbon beer cans. Eddie died at 45 years of age. Probably from alcohol. Mary and Aunt Helen died in the same month.

In 1979 Alvin sold the house in Pendleton. It was too much work to keep up and he knew Alan and I were not going to be farmers and work a corn field. We didn't want to live in the enchanted forest. Our futures were not going to be living in the country with a house with a nice lawn, good job, classy looking wife. The bourgeois life was out the window.

My parents could see how committed we were to becoming musicians and that we needed to be in the big city. We moved to Kenmore!

Alvin and Florence on their wedding day. Buffalo, 1952.

Florence Alvin Buffalo 1956

6357 Main Road Pendelton

Mary   Aunt Helen Alan   1957

HEY AUNT HELEN ! - 27

Grandma Loszka   Grandma Kalick
Alan Kevin   Pendelton NY 196

K cowboys - Pendleton 1965

28 - **KEVIN K**

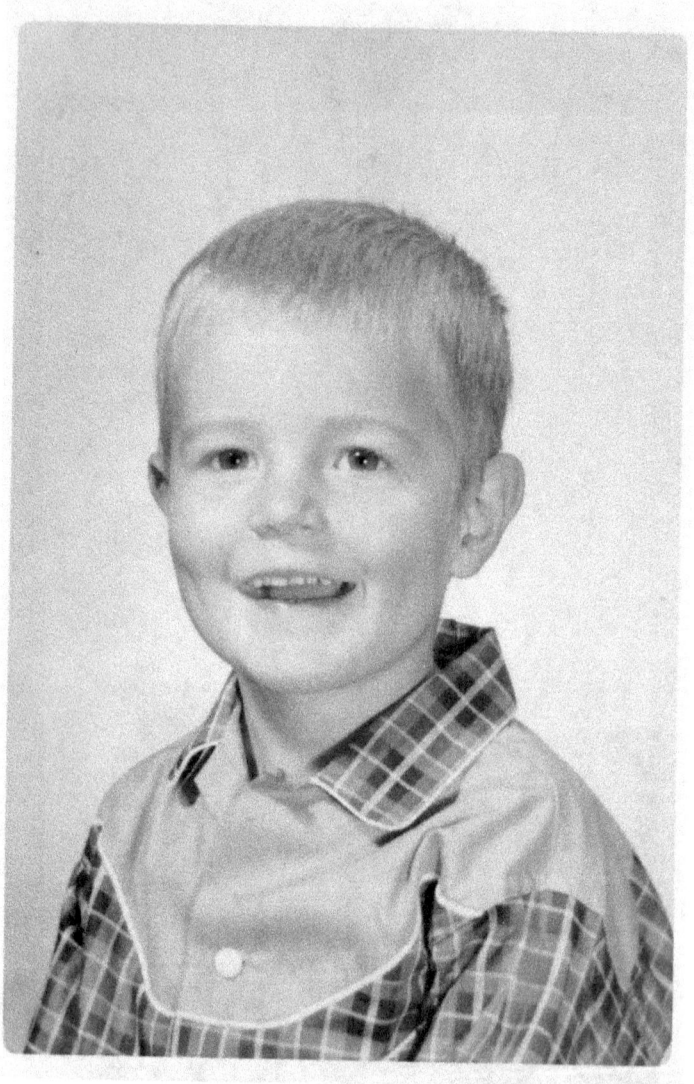

Alan

Kevin

Kalicki Brothers   Monk Brothers 1962

Kalicki car   1967

Alan in 1968

Christmas 1969

Pendelton Panther

Kevin Alvin Alan

Kevin   Alan   Bernice   Florence   1968

Kenan Center Lockport 1969

34 - KEVIN K

Kevin 1969

Kalicki Brothers 1975

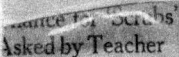

...ance ... Scrubs" Asked by Teacher

Is winning in sports so very important? I would say yes if on a professional level. It is logical that only the best players should be used. This is survival of the fittest.

Can this thinking be applied to children 14 and younger? It is frustrating and sad to see amateur hockey being played in the Lockport area, utilizing only the so-called best players. I had the impression that at this early age, every boy would be given the opportunity to play.

We all know that it is impossible to become proficient in any sport unless given the opportunity to at least try. I have observed as many as ten lonely-looking boys just waiting for the coach to let them play. I give these boys a lot of credit because it takes more than just guts to sit through game after game, completely ignored by the coach.

The so-called best players keep going in and out of the game, having a wonderful time while the scrubs keep warming the bench.

I am writing about this situation not only because my sons are scrubs, but because as a high school teacher I am involved with boys every day and my primary objective is to help every one of my students attain the highest possible level of learning.

It would indeed be sad if I were to concentrate on only the brighter students, and ignore completely the average or below average student. Is being a coach on a hockey team so much more difficult or different than being a school teacher? Why not spend more time with the scrub or at least give him some encouragement?

It would be interesting to know what the sponsors think. Being business people in most instances, I venture to guess that they would like to see all of the boys play.

Or is winning the most important thing after all?

I sincerely hope that only Lockport is guilty of such a situation and that this is not a general practice in other areas.

ALVIN R. KALICKI
Lockport, N.Y.

This is a letter Alvin wrote to the Lockport newspaper about me not having enough ice-time at the rink.

| 7 |

AUNT HELEN 1977

The year was 1977 when we formed our first real band. We named it Aunt Helen because we all had Aunt Helens. It was Kevin Rat on drums, Rocky Starr on guitar and vocals, Mr. Lunch on bass and vocals, and Zee on guitar. We loved the Sex Pistols, New York Dolls, Johnny Thunders, Dead Boys and the Ramones. We also liked King Crimson, Mahogany Rush, Ground Hogs and Five Dollar Shoes. We had a manager, John Titak, who would book us some good shows, and some weird shows too. We played a lot in the towns of Tonawanda and Lockport.

The scariest show we ever played was on an American Indian reservation in southern New York state. It was the Cattaraugus Reservation. We pulled up in our twenty-four-foot truck with a Marshall stack, SVT bass amp, double drum set and four PA cabinets, plus a full light show. At that time, we were doing three sets a night.

First set is KISS in complete makeup. Second set is the

Alice Cooper show with Alan in full makeup. Third set is the punk rock set. The club is packed with about 100 fully drunk Indians. The KISS set goes over well. We open with *Detroit Rock City*. We even had the explosions and fog machine at the end of the set. We go down to the basement. We get changed into our Alice Cooper show. In fact, Alvin had built us an electric chair. He built it from wood he bought at Sadlo Lumber Company. It was made from big, strong two by fours that are used in the foundations for houses. He even installed colored lights on top of it. Belts were used on the arms of the chair to tie Alan in it. How many kids' fathers built them an electric chair? Probably not many in Pendleton. Problem was it was too heavy to bring to the club.

Alvin also built four A-7 PA cabinets that each looked like a refrigerator and weighed 65 pounds each. They were painted white. Two giant horns on top that weighed 30 pounds each. We had two seven-foot-tall lighting trees with spotlights attached. Alan made a control board that was like the size of a stove, which had wiring in it. The lights were operated by standard light switches. We bought gun powder for our exploding boxes for the end of *Firehouse*.

My parents should have worked for KISS. Mother K could have made for Gene Simmons all his bat outfits and my father could have made all of Paul Stanley's empty Marshall cabinets. We also thought about making a giant tube of toothpaste. We were going to use a tube from a giant tractor tire. Never happened.

So, I have my face painted completely white and am wearing a prison outfit that Florence made. Alan has his face painted like the Alice Cooper record *Killer*. We start with *Under My Wheels*, *Billion Dollar Babies*, *I'm Eighteen*, *Shoe Salesman* and *Is It My Body*. When we get to *Dead Babies*, Alan is sharpening an axe with a grinder we had on stage to chop the plastic baby's head off at the end of the song. The audience doesn't understand what they are seeing. Alan brings the hatchet down on the baby's head and it goes flying onto the bar and almost into one of the Indians pitchers of Stroh's beer. We end the set and its completely quiet. Then we hear someone yell from the bar, 'Scalp 'em!' 'What?' We ran down into the basement where the dressing room was located. About five minutes later the owner comes down and says, 'Leave now, do not pack your gear. There is a back door. Use it. These Indians are completely drunk and want to hurt you all. They don't understand what Alice Cooper is.' He gave us our $300. We get outside. There is a fight going on with about ten guys who are all six-foot five and 300 pounds. We speed out of there and onto the highway back to Pendleton.

I'm with Alan and we are driving in his 1965 Volkswagen with his face still painted like Alice Cooper. Its winter, and the car has no heater for the almost two-hour ride back home. I also have on my prison outfit with no underwear. What if we had of been stopped by the police and ended up in jail way out in this *Deliverance* part of New York State? It would not have ended well for us.

The next day we go back to pick up our gear. We see two Sheriff patrol cars and crime tape around the whole front of the club. The owner tells us that after we left, the fight got even bigger, and when the police got there to break it up, they found a guy sitting in his car stabbed to death! We packed up all our gear and the owner says, 'Hey, a lot of the Indians liked you guys. Maybe soon we can set up another show?' We told our manager, John Titak the story and he just laughed and said, 'Do you have my twenty percent?' That's show business.

We, as Aunt Helen, agree to never again play on an Indian reservation. Not good for our careers.

The Aunt Helen Band has been rocking crowds in the Buffalo, N.Y. area recently. Pictured (L to␣␣R) K.K., drums

| 8 |

RECORDING OF BIG MONEY / REBECCA 7-INCH SINGLE

Right from the beginning, Aunt Helen always wrote songs. Alan had taken guitar lessons for ten years and the bass player Mr. Lunch had too. I was in the Starpoint School Band. They let me hit the big bass drum. I hated it. I wanted to be like Cozy Powell or Peter Criss. Aunt Helen had lots of songs: *Gestapo Capers, Box Lunch, Lance It, I Wanna Be Ed McMahon, Lester the Molester, Clean, Young and Pink, I Was A Teenage Pig* and *Baby, Is This The Wire From Your Braces?*

For our first single, we decided on *Big Money*, a song about a guy who has a job in a bank but has no life, and *Rebecca*, a song about a lesbian. I did not even know what a lesbian was.

Anyhow, we found the only studio in our area. It was in a town named Sanborn, NY. Just a stone building with no windows, and out in a cornfield. We brought in Alan's full 200-watt Marshall stack, SVT bass amp, Orange amp and my ten-piece double drum set. We knew zero about recording. I think there were two mics on the drums. We told the studio engineer that one song was about a lesbian. He didn't know what a lesbian was either. Anyway, we did it, and we were the first punk band in Upstate New York to release a single. It got a really good review in *Rock Scene* magazine from Lenny Kaye. We then got lots of mail to our house at 6357 Main Road. This is where we got the letter from GG Allin who loved *Big Money*.

My father Alvin printed all the covers for the single at his job at a drafting company named Finastra. Alvin worked with some crazy guys. A Canadian guy named Nick Julie who would use the expression, 'I don't give a care'. His boss was a guy named Joe Miller. He was mean. Alvin would be standing up at his desk, drawing air conditioner systems. Joe would always be bending over right in front of Alvin. He smelled. One day Alvin blew up and said, 'Joe, stop bending over in front of me. I can smell your ass!' At night, Alvin taught vocational drafting at Burgard High School. This school was in a bad neighborhood in Buffalo. It was on Kensington Avenue. There were always fights and stabbings. Mr. Visconi was the Principal, and Alvin told me he had a billy club that he carried, kind of like a small baseball bat. If he saw someone fighting, he would come out swinging the club. Cleared the room fast. They would take knives away from the students almost every day.

I never knew why but after about one year, Alvin retired

from teaching. He would bring home some of his students drawings to grade. I saw some. The kids he was teaching were around seventeen years old, yet the artwork they produced looked like something a ten year old would do. Very few had any interest in advancement. This one kid named Wilber Gofarb, he was a star on the basketball team, but as a student he had the IQ of a golf ball. I think that's why Alvin quit, plus I'm sure he was threatened.

Alvin would also print up our Aunt Helen fanzine at this job. We would come in late at night and run the Xerox machine until it was out of ink.

Alan in the studio recording 'Big Money'

Alan and I not only knew a lot about punk rock music but also about politics and the Hollywood scene. I think it came from watching Johnny Carson. The jokes were just so funny. There were no boundaries. Watching Shecky Greene or Don Rickles or Rodney Dangerfield. We were learning from professional joke tellers. I remember a Carson show where his guest was actress Dyan Cannon, a hot looking woman. She walked out onto the set and sat down with her cat on her lap. Great set up for Carson. Dyan says, 'Johnny, do you want to pat my pussy?' And Carson says, 'Sure. Move the cat!'

So, after putting all the pages of the fanzine together, we would drop some off at House of Guitars in Rochester. Greg Prevost from The Chesterfield Kings worked there. He was an Aunt Helen fan. Greg was the first person to stock the *Big Money* single.

It amazes me because even though we were just out of high school, we knew what we wanted. We had a plan, and it wasn't to buy a new tractor!

| 9 |

1972 CADILLAC

In 1980, Alan had a killer white 1972 Cadillac. Fantastic car to ride in. I felt like John Gotti. The first Toys rehearsal we had was at Doug

Tyler's house in Lewiston, NY. It was a long drive from our apartment in Tonawanda on Robert Drive.

Alan had a job as a dishwasher at an Italian restaurant on Niagara Falls Boulevard. The owners were, as they say, 'part of the family'. They liked Alan a lot. Once, we were late getting to rehearsal and we were going fast. *Really* fast. Speeding through stop signs and passing cars, Alan was driving like Dale Earnhardt (the father not the son). As we pulled into Doug's driveway, I opened the door and heard, 'Stay inside the car and don't move.' It was the Lewiston Police and they had us blocked in from behind. They pulled Alan out and put him against the back of the car, frisked him and asked him why he was driving so crazy because, 'We can put you in jail right now.' They said he was going 85 in a 35-mph school zone. After about an hour, the police decide to write tickets. They wrote up at least five tickets, over $1000 worth, and gave Alan a court date.

We had a good rehearsal. Right in the living room and a nice, isolated environment to work on *Instant Suicide* and *I'm a Non-Dairy Creamer*. Anyhow, the next day Alan went to work and showed his boss all the tickets. His boss said, 'No problems, we will take care of it.' And they did! Alan paid no money for the tickets and didn't even have to appear in court. It's good to know people in higher places. The law can be such a deterrent to young artists.

| 10 |

TOYS WILL DESTROY

At his show at The Continental in Buffalo, Johnny Thunders once said over the microphone, 'Hey, so tell me about these fried chicken wings. I also heard some strange things about a place called Kenmore, 80 Harrison Avenue.' This was the city and the address where we got serious about our music.

Aunt Helen ended. Tom the bass player was going to college. I can't fully remember the reason why we broke up, but we did. Never did any reunion shows either.

With Meat Cleaver and Doug Tyler, we knew we had the team to complete our mission. All the rehearsals were held in our basement. Small room but effective. The Toys had a strong degree in concentration to give our music something fanciful. Alvin installed some walls and insulation on the windows. We were concerned because the guy who lived next door was a prison guard. I was sure that there were many weapons in his house. I was also sure he probably didn't want to hear *Instant Suicide* or *Mutilation Boogie* after 9:00 PM. That's when these songs sound the best – like a hallucination.

It turned out that this guy's brother was Tony. Tony was a Toys fan who would come and see us all the time. He would wear a dress sometimes. He looked good. I think his look involved a beard too. It was in style for 1979 punk rock.

Doug and Meat were living in an apartment in Niagara Falls on Robinson Court. They met through a guitarist named Tim Donahue around 1976. They had a band named The Circle's End. The Toys sound man, Mike Fechner was on second guitar. After that, it was a band called Space Junk. Alan and I had a band with Doug right before Aunt Helen, called Grim Reaper. We played only a few shows. That was it.

There was a club we played a few times in Doug and Meat's neighborhood called Shutters and Boards. The whole dance floor was a checkerboard in black and white. The rumor was that Cheap Trick guitarist Rick Nielsen took that idea and used it on his guitar and straps. I guess Cheap Trick played there in the early 70's.

It was kind of a long drive to Kenmore for Doug and Cleaver but there was always a beer supply in the back seat. We always used to rehearse at night. Meat Cleaver was always ambitious after coming home from Twin Fare. This is where he got a butcher's outfit to wear on stage. Just a colossal idea. I remember spending a whole week practicing standing on my drums and playing. I would have one foot on my drum seat and the other foot on the floor tom tom. I would continue the beat on the snare and cymbal. The moment was in the guitar solo of Doug's song *Come With Me*. I can guarantee the drummer from Rush never practiced that!

We played fast and hard. It was a great time for music in 1979-82. We saw The Police at Stage One in front of fifty people. We also saw U2, the Dead Boys, Ramones and Thunders in Rochester and with Jerry Nolan at Scorgies. There was a girl named Mary who was the sound engineer there. She always wanted a three way with Alan and me.

Our favorite radio station was CFNY 102.1 from Toronto. This was where we heard all the punk rock and power pop songs. Lots of inspiration to write. The Toys had great songs like *Mutilation Boogie, Broken Glass, Instant Suicide, FYYB, Mondo TV, Livin' Fast, Self-Abuse, Pauline, Don't Know Why, Delirious, 666 and I'm a Mutant.*

My brother had a girlfriend named Jeanette. She knew Eddie Tice from Harvey and Corkey Productions, the biggest management company in western New York. Yes, it's the same Harvey Weinstein. I think he was horny back then too. In fact, we all were. Don't forget it was part of being in show business in the 1980's.

Jeanette invited Eddie Tice to our show at McVans in Buffalo. This is the club where I saw the Dead Boys play in

1978. The night Stiv Bator peed in his hand and wiped it on his face. Never saw anyone do that before.

We were opening for Electro-Man. It was completely packed. The Toys played twelve songs without stopping. It was just a sweeping sound like Mongolian horsemen charging in with swords out, destroying everything in their way. A complete nihilistic performance. As dangerous as Castro pushing the buttons to launch misses at the U.S.A.

The Toys refused to be ignored. I have a cassette of the show and it is amazing. It sounds like we snorted a gram of speed. We left the audience stunned. When we went back to the dressing room, Eddie Tice came back to meet us. Told us we were great, and he would like to help manage us. That was it, as simple as that. No contract, just a handshake and a few drinks.

1980 was our first big show opening for Pat Benatar at Stage One. All the other Buffalo bands were jealous of The Toys because we could choose any show we wanted to open for. It was fair because Talas and us were the best bands in New York.

We continued playing every show in western New York. Also, many trips were made to Toronto. There was a great music scene in the 1980's there too.

When we opened for a band on Stiff Records called Dirty Looks, we made our first connection. Great guys, great songs. The two LP's they did are super cool. This band should have been huge. Their bass player Marco played in our band Lone Cowboys in 1987.

Their guitarist Patrick invited us to open for them a few times in NYC at the Peppermint Lounge. Their management company also booked us our first show at CBGB. This company was managing Grand Funk Railroad at the time.

Around 1981, Patrick said he wanted to produce an LP for us. He stayed at my brother's apartment in Amherst for one week. He changed some parts in our songs. Doug wasn't too happy when Patrick omitted the beginning part of the song *Say It*. The ten songs were recorded and mixed in one week.

The album entitled *Say It* came out super poppy. Patrick took a lot of dirt out of The Toys, and really cleaned us up. He said, 'Look, just make it sound like this so we can get the record deal. Then you can go back and record your own version of these songs. Make it back to the dirtier Toys.' I thought it was a smart move. Don't forget that whenever you get someone to produce your music it always changes. You become the vision of the producer and not yourself anymore.

Well, when *Say It* came out, our audience thought we had sold out to get a record deal. I can't argue with them. It didn't work. The whole atmosphere was changed. The life was sucked right out of our musical blimp. Meat Cleaver continued to do his 'Kenmore Roll' where he would jump into the audience and roll on the floor knocking people over. Kind of didn't work when we would be singing my pop song *Stay Away*. I felt progressively useless.

Then Dirty Looks broke up and their manager died. Welcome to the world of show business.

The Toys played sixty shows in 1980 and fifty-five in 1981. We did four shows with the Romantics in 1980. Buffalo, Rochester, Syracuse and Albany. Their guitar player, Wally Palmer thought Meat Cleaver was great. When he saw the butcher's outfit he was really impressed! Also, they both had Polish blood. I started setting up my tom toms flat like their drummer Jimmy Marinos. The band just had a cool look to them. The first time we played with the Romantics, they all had on black leather suits. Then the following year we opened for them and they all had on pink suits. Super cool.

The Romantics rode in a van that had four beds inside. The two managers, 'The Arties' rode in the front. They would play and after the show have a couple of beers, get in their van and drive that same night to the next city. All the gear with the roadies was in a separate truck. I could tell this band was going to become big. They knew how to work hard.

In 1981, The Toys travelled to Toronto to open for Teenage Head at the Horseshoe Club. Again, a cool band with great songs. Teenage Head would sometimes back Johnny Thunders.

The Fast came to Buffalo to play. It was the first band I ever met that had a female roadie. She was a girl who was super tough. Carried in the Marshall amps with no problems. She was from Brooklyn, of course.

We drove to NYC on March 12 to open for Bauhaus at a club called Privates. This was an odd show. The entire audience was Goth. Everybody was dressed like a bat or a vampire. I thought it was like *The Rocky Horror Picture Show*. The audience was polite for our set. The singer Peter Murphy was nice to talk to. This band became super huge in the 1980's.

We then went back to Toronto to open for The Diodes. Kind of like a Canadian version of the Romantics. They had a song called *Tired of Waking Up Tired* that was super catchy.

Detroit was the next stop. Nunzio's club was where Billy Idol's song *Dancing With Myself* premiered, right before our set. It was very exciting to hear it because we loved Generation X. We had heard they broke up and didn't think anything good could come from it. I was wrong.

We then played Detroit's famous club, Bookies. Gang War and Iggy played shows there in the early 1980's.

The dressing room was upstairs. We played a great set. There was a bartender named Animal. Animal really like me. Very friendly, dressed in a complete leather outfit like Rob Halford of Judas Priest. I had a few drinks with him and then escaped to the upstairs. Our gear was packed, we were ready to leave and then I heard, 'Kev, Kev, I'm waiting for you.' What? Animal was downstairs yelling up at me in the staircase.

I was getting a little nervous. There was an S&M shop next to the club. I think Animal wanted to take me over there and buy me some crotchless leather underwear. I told Animal, 'Thanks for everything, but we are like the Romantics, and are driving back to Buffalo after the show.' He accepted it. If I had of went with him, who knows, maybe I would have ended up playing drums for Gang War or Iggy Pop.

| 11 |

1976 BORN AGAIN PUNK

Alan and I always had good taste in music. We knew the players that were from a different world, like Hendrix, Keith Moon, Rory Gallagher. We knew it was impossible to achieve anything like these guys did. There was movement coming into our world.

1976, that was it. While shopping at House of Guitars in Rochester, Greg Prevost told us about bands like the Dead Boys. Their guitarist was a guy named Cheetah Chrome. And the Sex Pistols with a guy named Sid Vicious. And of course, Johnny Thunders.

We bought the 7-inch single of *God Save the Queen* and the *Young Loud and Snotty* LP. WOW, this was it! We had never experienced danger in music. I followed the Sex Pistols US tour through our

Buffalo evening newspaper with Irv Weinstein reporting each night on the shows in the South. Really exciting. So fresh and different. With safety pins too.

Then we heard that the Dead Boys were playing McVans in Buffalo. This was 1978. We get to the club and there are 200 people inside. The Dead Boys are on stage sound checking. Stiv and Cheetah were wearing matching leather jackets. So intense. We didn't even go close. They had that huge guy with them as their roadie, Merv I think his name was. About two hours later, the Dead Boys start the set with *Sonic Reducer* and then into *All This and More*. The energy level is unbelievable. Beer flings everywhere. Stiv puts his hand down his pants and pees in his hand, then proceeds to wipe it on his face. At the end of the set, Stiv beats himself with a chain. Never saw Billy Sheehan from Talas do that on stage.

Buffalo is well graced with **Aunt Helen**, composed of K.K.K., Zee, Rocky Starr, and Mr. Lunch. They have fanzines and a 45 available from Alan Kalicki, 6357 Main Road, Lockport, New York 14094. ☐

That year, we also saw Johnny Thunders at Scorgies in Rochester. I was right up front. Johnny had a Fender twin amp on a chair on full volume. Beneath the chair were shots of whiskey. Johnny must have changed his strings right before the show as he hadn't cut off the strings on the machine head of his beat-up Gibson guitar, so the strings poked me in the arm a few times. I mean I was 12 inches from him. The next day my teeth hurt as John's amp was so loud! It was just as we thought it would be. I love that memory.

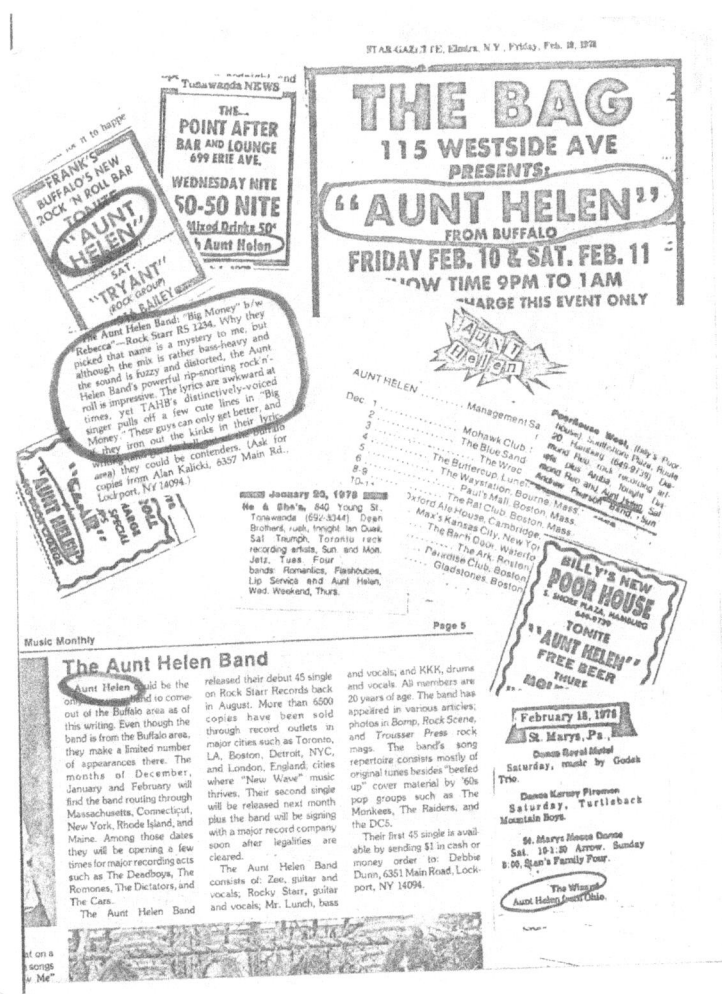

Aunt Helen fanzine #1

HEY AUNT HELEN ! - 57

Insert from the Big Money 7"

Aunt Helen - Big Money b/w Rebecca - 7" released in 1978

ALAN 1968

GRIM REAPER
BOB PAXON STEVEN OLICK JOHN BERG
KEVIN ALAN 1975
steeve died in france 1981

Alan as Alice 1977

HEY AUNT HELEN ! - 61

Aunt Helen as Kiss - Buffalo, 1976

62 - KEVIN K

Aunt Helen - Pendleton garage - 1977

Aunt Helen rehearsal - 1976

Kevin, Wayne Cozad, Florence, Alvin, Alan. Robert Drive apartment, 1979.

| 12 |

AUNT HELEN LYRICS

BIG MONEY

Rise and shine he is up by six
As he stumbles to the kitchen to get his bowl of Trix
Put on your leisure suit and conservative tie
Pinch your wife's ass and kiss her good bye
To make Big Money Big Money

Hop in your 1978 Corvette wow
He's on his way to watch the Dow
Stocks and Bonds is all you care about
Why should you care if your son flunks out
To make Big Money Big Money

Do you have someone working under you?
Why yes, a young secretary of twenty-two
Sex is on your mind and you can't fool her
Especially when you find her panties floating
in the water cooler

Solo

He wants to live high on the hog
And doesn't care if his family goes to the dogs
Stuff that lunch meat right down your face
I hope you choke fatso your [SIC] such a disgrace
To make Big Money Big Money

REBECCA

Well help me, help me, help me
She's driving me insane
Nobody takes little Becky out
But she never seems to complain

Now I was with your best friend
And like her I like your dark brown hair
I love your Italian cooking
And I love the clothes you wear
I'm gonna ask you to the movies I think
Je vais coucher avec toi ce coir
But she says no before the words leave my lips
Cousin Becky never gets too far

Rebecca when I realize the situation
Rebecca I wanted to laugh out loud
Rebecca now I know I was wasting my time
Rebecca oh no

You better you better you better
You better tell me who
Who's your mystery boyfriend Becky?
She's your best friend if I know you

Rebecca when I realize the situation
Rebecca I wanted to laugh out loud

Rebecca now I know I was wasting my time
Rebecca oh no

I know you think I'm crazy
Considering what I don't know
Then why don't you drop your silly friend
And come with me to the show
Becky, Becky, Becky
I can't believe how this can be
You're gonna drop this handsome guy
For this girl that I now see

I WAS A TEENAGE PIG

Didn't go to school didn't wash my tool
I was a teenage pig
Stayed on the farm I had no charm
I was a teenage pig

Pig I was a Teenage Pig

Always loved to flirt
Used to pull up my skirt
I was a Teenage Pig
I found my thrill
Then went on the Pill
I was a Teenage Pig

Pig I was a Teenage Pig

Off with me head
Wrap me in plastic
I was a Teenage Pig
Fry me in pan
I'll taste fantastic, because
I was Teenage Pig

LESTER THE MOLESTER

Been hangin' round the schoolyard since 12:36
Gonna find some cute kid and get my kicks
Recess in the playground at quarter after two
Come here little girl I gotta bag of candy of for you
He is Lester the Molester
He's got a surprise for you
He will take you for a joy ride
And he will rape you too

Not too young Not too shy
I like that girl with the big brown eyes
Long dark hair and cute little smile
Come here little pisspot I wanna hold you awhile
He is Lester the Molester

Hi there little girl you can call me Uncle Pervy
Here is my bag of candy I want to play dirty
I'll make sure to set you free
After you eat my Tootsie Roll that's attached to me
He is Lester the Molester
He's got a surprise for you
He will take you for a joy ride
And he will rape you too

THE WIRE FROM YOUR BRACES

Baby is this the wire from your braces?
Cause I found it in the sink today
Well I plugged into my radio
And the thing began to play

What am I gonna do about your braces?
What if you want them back?
What will I do about your braces?

Okay so it's not the wire from your braces
But I found this thing today
And I plugged it into my radio
And the thing began to play

CLEAN YOUNG AND PINK

Stopped without given a chance
I've tried so long to get into your pants
I like how you tease everyone with your wink
I like you 'cause you're Clean Young and Pink

You're Clean Young and Pink

Brush cut and a mustache
How can you like a guy like that?
You go outta your way to say hello
To that guy who looks like a snake he is so low

You're Clean Young and Pink

He's stupid with no personality
He will never be a great as me
You would rather do it with a schmuck on a farm
Than this perfect guy with lots of charm
You will then go around with a kid
Who is an ugly acned disgrace
When I see him I will spit at him
And call him Pizza Face

You're Clean Young and Pink

BOX LUNCH

She will let anyone enter her dress
Whatever you want the answer is yes
She didn't care if she was the talk of the town
You don't need an excuse to sleep on your own
Besides the guys won't leave you alone

How about inviting me over for lunch?
I could go for a nice Box Lunch

You are about to move away
Because you and your tits are now full grown
Then you entertain whenever you want
Soon you will be the talk of the town
And you will know deep down
All the fellows will want your nice Box Lunch

How about inviting me over for a nice Box Lunch?
I could go for a nice Box Lunch

There's ten guys outside your windowpane
Waitin' to pull the train
I wonder who will be the caboose?
Surely not me I don't like that bunch
I'm too full to have lunch
I laughed when the caboose was you

GESTAPO CAPERS

3rd Reich 3rd Reich

Munich beer cellar 11-9-23
Ambition to rule a little country
Few years later doing time in Lansperberg Prison
Gonna build an audience and they are gonna listen

Just got the morning paper
Headlines about a Gestapo Caper
The sound of hobnail boots
Marching down and old French street
All the French people
Looking out their windows in disbelief

Remember those warm Mediterranean nights?
Along the Riviera coast
Where we danced and danced toast after toast
Or do you remember you and me my dear
What a pair
Glaring at the bombs
The bombs bursting in air

The TOYS first promo photo 1979

Alan .. Meat Cleaver .. Eddie Tice .. Kevin 1980

HEY AUNT HELEN! - 77

The TOYS 1981

The TOYS McVans Buffalo 1980

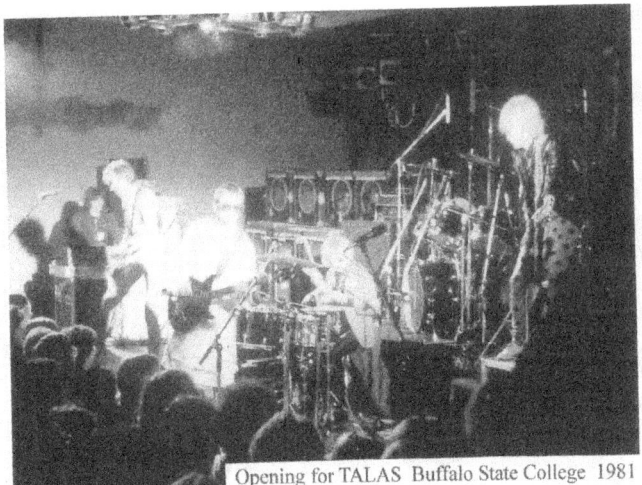

Opening for TALAS Buffalo State College 1981

HEY AUNT HELEN! - 81

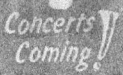

THE ROMANTICS / THE TOYS
January 27
Harvey & Corky's Stage 1

Most people have probably lost count of how many times The Romantics have come to this area as an opening act. But with their latest appearance at Stage 1, the stage, the ding beat between numbers. After racing through "Hung On You," and "Gimme One More Chance," the pace slowed to a contented clip as bassist Rich Cole stepped up to sing "I Can't Wait Till I see You Again."

As the set progressed one couldn't help but get lost in the positive rock and roll attitude projected by The Romantics. These guys would be perfect for a 1980 remake of *A Hard Day's Night*.

The band played their two independently-produced singles, "Tell It to Carrie" and "Little White Lies," followed by Marlon's classic vocals on the new one, "What I Like About You." An encore of the Stones' "The Last Time" signaled the end of the show, and probably the end of The Romantics' club touring days. This band is set to score it big.

The Toys should be able to take heart watching The Romantics' impending explosion. Their opening set was nearly as exciting as the visiting Detroiters' and the fans are increasing in number all the time.

Not many local bands can make the dancers hit the floor on the first note, but their originals "Instant Suicide," "Living Past" and "Mutilation Boogie" got the muscles moving in a hurry.

The band played a few new numbers in addition to their already solid original set. Guitarist Mick Tyler's "Self Abuse" and Kevin Reid's remake of "One Fine Day" will be popular additions to their remaining outings.

82 - KEVIN K

HEY AUNT HELEN ! - 83

MAY 1982
bookie's Club 870

870 W. MCNICHOLS · DETROIT
2½ blocks west of Woodward
862-0877   862-0816

DESIGN—MATTHEW ROSS

thursday	friday	saturday
		1 ROUGH CUT plus GUEST BAND
6 NOBODY'S CHILDREN & THE OTTERS	7 RAY GUNN TAZE also CUTBACKS	8 3-D INVISIBLES & THE IN
13 NON FICTION & BOULDER	14 INSECT SURFERS FROM VIRGINIA with THE END	15 NEW TOYS FROM N.Y. & PAPER HEARTS
20 PRIVATE ANGST & VEE TOPS	21 FLIRT also FLEXIBLES	22 BLACK MARKET MIKE GOULD & THE GENE PERL BAND
27 DEMANDS and GUILTY	28 BROKEN ENGLISH FROM CHICAGO & THE LOADZ	29 KEVIN LEE & THE HEART BEAT SPUTNIKS

SureShot

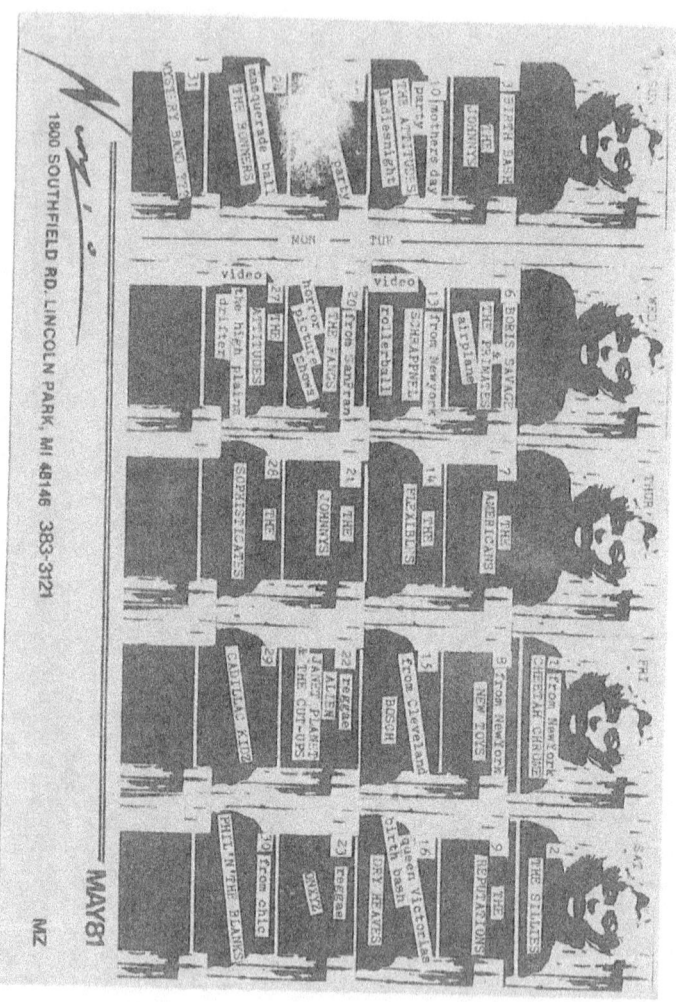

HEY AUNT HELEN ! - 85

Friday, March 6, 1981
The Buffalo Evening News/Gusto

HEY AUNT HELEN ! - 87

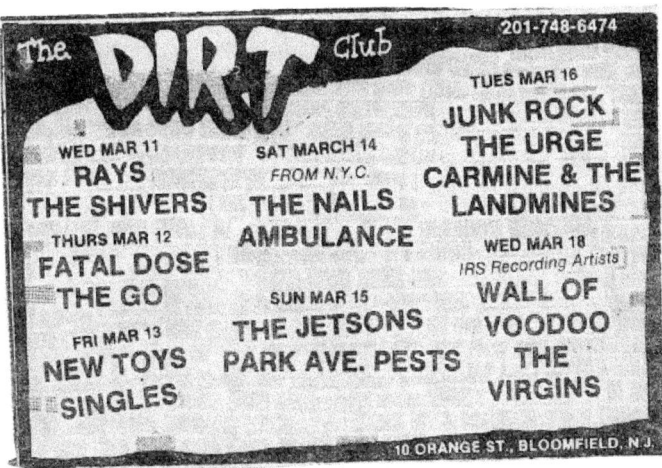

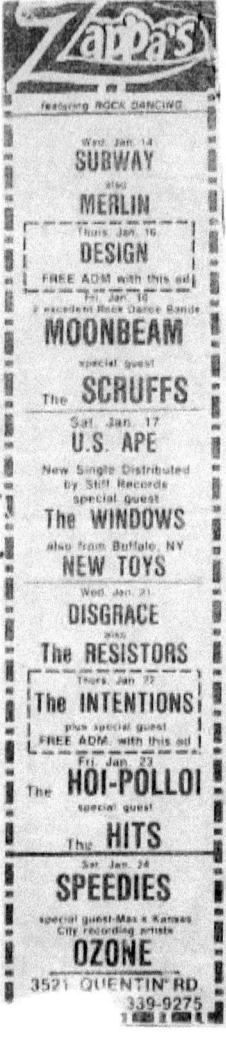

HEY AUNT HELEN! - 91

New Toys - 1982

HEY AUNT HELEN ! - 93

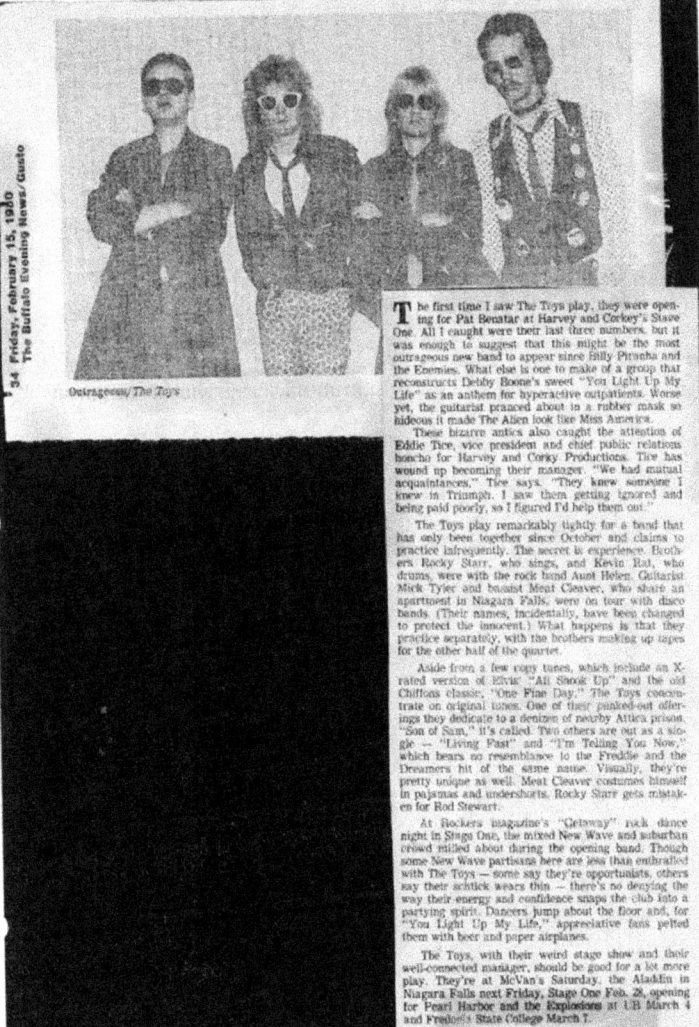

34 Friday, February 15, 1980 — The Buffalo Evening News/Gusto

Outrageous/The Toys

The first time I saw The Toys play, they were opening for Pat Benatar at Harvey and Corky's Stage One. All I caught were their last three numbers, but it was enough to suggest that this might be the most outrageous new band to appear since Billy Piranha and the Enemies. What else is one to make of a group that reconstructs Debby Boone's sweet "You Light Up My Life" as an anthem for hyperactive outpatients. Worse yet, the guitarist pranced about in a rubber mask so hideous it made The Alien look like Miss America.

These bizarre antics also caught the attention of Eddie Tice, vice president and chief public relations honcho for Harvey and Corky Productions. Tice has wound up becoming their manager. "We had mutual acquaintances," Tice says. "They knew someone I knew in Triumph. I saw them getting ignored and being paid poorly, so I figured I'd help them out."

The Toys play remarkably tightly for a band that has only been together since October and claims to practice infrequently. The secret is experience. Brothers Rocky Starr, who sings, and Kevin Rat, who drums, were with the rock band Aunt Helen. Guitarist Mick Tyler and bassist Meat Cleaver, who share an apartment in Niagara Falls, were on tour with disco bands. (Their names, incidentally, have been changed to protect the innocent.) What happens is that they practice separately, with the brothers making up tapes for the other half of the quartet.

Aside from a few copy tunes, which include an X-rated version of Elvis' "All Shook Up" and the old Chiffons classic, "One Fine Day," The Toys concentrate on original tunes. One of their pinked-out offerings they dedicate to a denizen of nearby Attica prison. "Son of Sam," it's called. Two others are out as a single — "Living Fast" and "I'm Telling You Now," which bears no resemblance to the Freddie and the Dreamers hit of the same name. Visually, they're pretty unique as well. Meat Cleaver costumes himself in pajamas and undershorts. Rocky Starr gets mistaken for Rod Stewart.

At Rockers magazine's "Getaway" rock dance night in Stage One, the mixed New Wave and suburban crowd milled about during the opening band. Though some New Wave partisans here are less than enthralled with The Toys — some say they're opportunists, others say their schtick wears thin — there's no denying the way their energy and confidence snaps the club into a partying spirit. Dancers jump about the floor and, for "You Light Up My Life," appreciative fans pelted them with beer and paper airplanes.

The Toys, with their weird stage show and their well-connected manager, should be good for a lot more play. They're at McVan's Saturday, the Aladdin in Niagara Falls next Friday, Stage One Feb. 28, opening for Pearl Harbor and the Explosions at UB March 4 and Fredonia State College March 7.

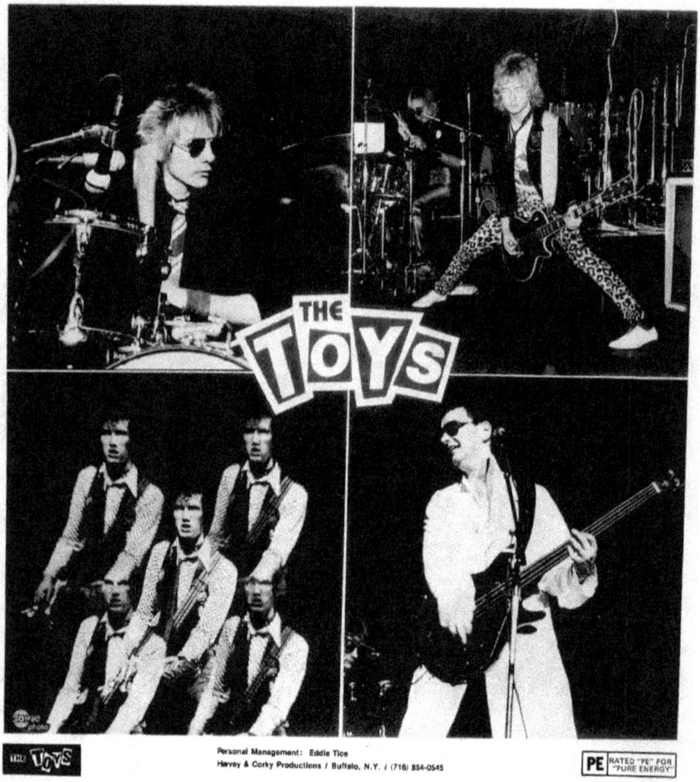
THE TOYS
THE TOYS
Personal Management: Eddie Tice
Harvey & Corky Productions / Buffalo, N.Y. / (716) 854-0545
PE
RATED "PE" FOR "PURE ENERGY"

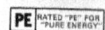

HEY AUNT HELEN ! - 97

Continental, Buffalo - 1982

HEY AUNT HELEN! - 99

Talas plays second to Toys, punk meets heavy metal

by J. Matthew Moravec
LEADER Staff Writer

FREDONIA COLLEGE
SEP 19, 80.

Two of Buffalo's most successful rock bands, Talas and the Toys, brought their oddly-matched brands of metal machine music to the Campus Center Friday night. Though the show was far from flawless, live music is to be welcomed whenever the people from UBG can provide it.

The Toys, a decidedly colorful quasi-punk group, opened with *Box Lunch*, a tune from their arsenal of originals. The originals borrow from the music and bad taste humor of the Knack.

Mick, the lead guitarist, looking a bit like Chevy Chase or some lost little boy, even sneered a la Doug Fieger from time to time. Song titles like *Self Abuse* and *Instant Suicide* strike me as being really juvenile. Mick defended them later, explaining that he hates love songs and predictability.

Even with Mick's amp disabled through much of the show, the Toys played some superb raunch'n'roll. The drummer slashed diagonally with his right arm (with a mechanical precision Charlie Watts-style); his brother, the rhythm guitarist had a Rod Stewart shag and sang like Wreckless Eric (including Cockney accent); and Meat Cleaver, a mechanical mesomorph of a bassist, fired off some lightning riffs. Their obscene gesturing and ludicrous lyrics made one forget about their fine musicianship. Unfortunately, they were not appreciated by the audience, who threw toilet paper and shouted "Talas!" at every opportunity.

The "" vs finished their performance with their own harmonied *Delirious*, the mid-60's classic, *Red Rubber Ball*, and a cooking *Slow Down*. Meat Cleaver halted the show abruptly by uttering "Fuck you!" and "Good night!" in the same breath.

What? No "God Save the Queen" or "You Light Up My Life"?

"No," Mick replied, "We had to cut out covers of recent songs."

I asked Meat Cleaver, a fairly friendly fellow actually, "Hey, where do you think you guys are going?"

He answered without hesitation, "To the top! To the top!"

Talas has been around...oh God, too long! playing an even mixture of covers and originals, this three-man act is about as exciting as clipped toenails. They always seem to take something out of the covers and there is *nothing* to take out of the originals.

Bill Sheehan may be a flashy bassist, playing overhand (gasp!) and with his elbows (gee whiz!), but Talas has absolutely no sense of tension or spontaneity so critical in even mediocre rock'n'roll. Their attempts at New Wave songs like *I'm the Man* and *Can't Stand Loving You* were futile.

Their new album is being produced by a man whose knack for good songwriting is almost as lacking as their own. *Seesaw* is the poorest excuse for a song I've ever heard. The only song they did not butcher was Montrose's great *Rock Candy*.

The crowd thinned out after the first set, so maybe downtown proved more attractive than the guys from Talas shaking outdated hairstyles around. Well, at least the first half of this production was entertaining. Let's hope for more, and better music in the future.

Talas bassist Bill Sheehan

McVans, Buffalo, 1980

The Toys - Aladdin Club, Niagara Falls 1980

scorgies

150 Andrews St • 232-9661

As Kevin Patrick, lead singer of New Math and WCMF DJ says: "The only club that matters." We go nationwide to provide you with all the best in local and national acts!

We are Proud to present three very special reggae events!

I-TAL
From Cleveland, Ohio!

CRUCIAL REGGAE and RUBADUB
Fri-Sat DEC 11-12 adm $4.00

The Rastafarians
from Santa Cruz, California

California's Premier Reggae Group
WED DEC 23!

SAT DEC 19: $1 Admission! By Your Request! **JAH EARL** the Premier Reggae DJ in Town will play your favorite music all nite! It's a Reggae Dance Party!

THE DRONGOS
from NEW ZEALAND!
appearing with the CLICHES!

THURS DEC 10
definitely not a clone band!
The Drongos will provide you with a
TWO FULL!! Sets of original, moveable music!

The NEW TOYS
from Buffalo, New York!

w/ Don't Call Me Junior on Thurs DEC 17
(established Rochester musicians playing a rock-a-billy, danceable style of music in their 1st public appearance)
w/ DelRoy ReBop Fri DEC 18!
(and they don't need a description!!)

| 13 |

MARK FREELAND

Mark was probably the most colorful and creative of Buffalo musicians. He had the band Electro Man and a punk rock band called The Fems. The Fems had a funny song called *Go To A Party and Act Like an Asshole.* They had a Public Image Ltd. kind of sound.

Here is a story about Mark as told by Doug Tyler of The Toys.

'I was working at Record Theatre on Main Street in Buffalo. Mark was buying a record and was like 27 cents short. There was a woman and her young son in line behind him. He asked the woman for change and she said, 'NO'. Mark said something about her being rich, so why couldn't she give him the money? Then he saw me and said, 'Hey Aunt Helen, you got 27 cents?' So I gave it to him just to get out of the store.'

| 14 |

BAD BEHAVIOR

1984 and it's another band for Alan and me. Lone Cowboys. Firstly with Peter Cain on bass, then with Marco Sin on bass from Dirty Looks.

Just like The Toys who had great songs, Lone Cowboys recorded *You Light Up My Life*, the Debby Boone hit from 1977. We sold thousands of that single. Lone Cowboys had a lot of great songs. Our sound was like The Church, Echo and the Bunnymen, and Lords of the New Church.

We were number one on many college radio stations. Yet little by little drugs became just as important as the music. In 1988, we had no proper record deal. So, another change came.

In 1989 it was Road Vultures. We were bad news right from the start. Alan's focus was chasing drugs and my main focus was chasing girls.

Distractions, not good for music. No turning back. We surrounded ourselves with all the bad elements of the NYC music scene.

Road Vultures

| 15 |

A-OK

In 1989 Alan was working for The Sockman. It was an outside stand that sold socks and gloves and was located right below Sounds record store. Alan would set them up early. He saw Johnny Thunders many times up at 7:00 AM walking down St. Marks Place. Thunders had probably been up all-night doing drugs somewhere. At night around 8:00 PM, it would be time for Alan to take everything down.

The owner of the storefront where the stand was located never let anyone use their toilet. Alan said that one time in the morning he had to 'let the kids off at the pool', but he had no toilet. He saw someone coming out of the store and they held the door open for Alan. So, he went to the toilet (that no one was allowed to use) and took a dump into a brown paper bag and left it on top of the toilet. Bon Appetite.

In 1995, while Alan and I were living at 23 Lexington Ave, The George Washington Hotel, he would walk the streets every night looking though garbage cans. He would always find something cool. Lots of clothes and food. Alan knew that at 10:00 PM, the bagel place across the street would empty out their old bagels. So every morning, we had stale bagels.

One evening, I came home late. I opened the refrigerator and inside was a whole wedding cake. I don't know where you would find an entire wedding cake but there it was. When Alan came home, he said, 'Did you see the cake I found?' Yes, I did. He was very proud of that find.

Alan always thought it was a big deal going to buy drugs with Johnny Thunders. They would meet at 13th Street and 2nd Ave and then head east down to Ave C. It was like a game. The copping and not getting arrested was almost a bigger high than doing the drugs. From what I heard, Alan had some clients who had very good jobs but didn't want to risk getting arrested. Alan had no fear at all of the police.

Alan would find five people each to give him $20. Then he would buy what was known as a bundle of dope. I think it's ten bags. Alan's pay was a free bag. Alan told me that Thunders had a small pocket sewed under his zipper on his pants where, after making a buy, he would slip the bags in there. If he was stopped by the police and frisked, it would have never been found. For Alan, this type of life became his full-time business. Kind of like playing by the railroad tracks. My father used to ask Alan, 'Why are you using drugs now in your life when you are older and smarter?' Alan would say, 'Well, Jerry Nolan was in his forties when he became a junkie.' Alan also used to cut all the tops off his t-shirts around the neck. Again, Alvin would ask, 'Why are all your t-shirts cut?' Alan would say, 'Because that is what Cheetah Chrome did to his shirts.' Nothing funny in these stories.

There is a sketch which Alan did of Johnny Thunders apartment. The day before, Alan was with John buying drugs. They came back to our 13th street apartment. This is when John picked up my Silvertone guitar and sang a new song called 'Disappointed In You'. Then Alan and John went back to his apartment he was renting from a girl on 21st street, right across the street from a police station - typical.

The next day Alan told me about Johnny's apartment being a complete mess, clothes and live cassettes everywhere. Alan also saw the yellow Gibson guitar on the floor, the one Dee Dee Ramone broke. Alan asked John, why doesn't he get it fixed and he said 'No it's broken for good.' He probably would have sold it to Alan for $100. There were also blood streaks on the wall of the bathroom and empty dope bags on the floor. That's when Alan sketched out the layout of JT's apartment. This was the last place Mr. Thunders lived before leaving for Japan and then ending up in New Orleans.

| 16 |

RIDE ON WITH ALAN K

When Alan heard the Thunders tune *Blame It On Mom*, he immediately said, 'We have to write a song with two chords.' Because *Blame It On Mom* was two chords, A and D, we spent many days, and then Alan finally had it, *Fire It Up*, but with three chords. This was in 1987 and the plan was to get John to play on the recording, but that never happened. Cheetah was always around, so he played on it.

We kept a Fostex cassette recorder at my parents' house in Florida. This was 1989-94. Alan would leave NYC for a vacation, stay with my parents and work on songs. Then when he came back to NYC, I would fly down and vacation and listen to what Alan had recorded and then add my own parts like harmony vocals or rhythm guitar. This system always worked well because then we would never argue about song structure. With my songs, *Scissors* and *Rosalene,* Alan changed a lot of the lyrics on both of these and gave them that desperate feel. Alan was desperate then too. He loved the Road Vultures song *More* because I wrote it about River Phoenix who had died from an overdose in front of the Viper Room in Hollywood.

When Kurt Cobain died the *New York Post* newspaper had a photo of Kobain with a shotgun on his mouth on the front page. Alan had that photo taped on the living room wall of our 13th Street apartment.

The *Ride* CD was completely written using the Fostex cassette player. I also remember Alan had a plastic container filled with rice to use as a shaker on *Cherry Vanilla*. He also had a poster roll about 12 inches long, and he put the microphone at the end of it which made a little reverb! That's amazing if I think about that now.

The song *Burn* was about the LA riots. Alan was very creative with his lyrics. For sure, the drugs he took enhanced the performance. Alan used to tell me, 'Keith Richards said take any drugs or drink whatever you need to get you into the frame of mind for writing or recording!'

That last song on the *Ride* CD, Alan wrote about the girl he used to buy drugs from in Hollywood. Those little keyboard parts were done on a $25 Casio keyboard that I still have. It also still has the tape on the keys of what notes to play. And again, on the bonus song on the *Ride* CD with Jerry Nolan leaving phone messages, the music is from that Casio keyboard.

I kind of knew that maybe this was the last adventure for Alan with recording. Alan's life was played out in all of his songs from start to finish. He was great at painting the picture of his songs. Never would hide his feelings. Very personal.

I know Alan would hate the world we are in now. I surely do. In the last six months I have been using the Keith Richards five-string open G tuning method to writing new songs. This is really fun for me. That's why I am using the name 'Cadallac Kevin'. I told the guys at the grocery store I was gonna have business cards made up with 'Kevin K – The Cadallac Of Men' printed on them. They thought that was funny and now call me that name.

What's strange is that I remember Alan showing me the opening guitar riff to the Stones *Rocks Off.* Alan and Alvin are still walking next to me every day.

Kevin and Alan, Continental Divide, NYC, 1989

116 - KEVIN K

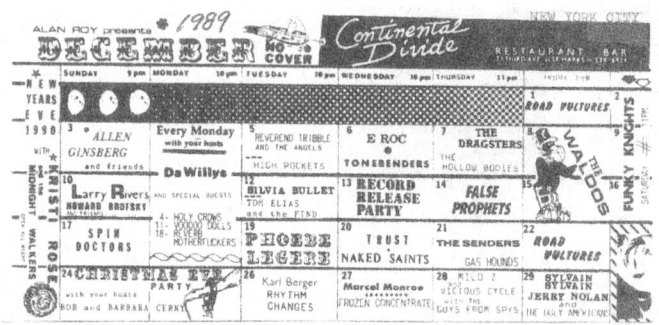

Circumstantial Records Presents

ROAD VULTURES

Debut Release
"FIRE IT UP"

Downtown rock and balls from the Road Vultures, restoring trash pop for the masses. Features ex-Dead Boy Cheetah Chrome on three tracks! The hope and glory of NYC rock returns!

AVAILABLE AT:
Tower, HMV, Kim's Underground,
St. Marks Sounds, and all fine stores

FOR MAIL ORDER INFO:
Circumstantial Records
12 Seventh Avenue
Brooklyn, NY 11217

SOUND VIEWS 23

Road Vultures hit Atlantis Feb. 19th, and all we can say is: New York Dolls/ Faster Pussycat fans gather round! Unfortunately only two or three did stay to see the dudes with feather hats… and fishnets bridging the rips in their jeans. (Now don't go getting all wet.)

This kind of music thrives on simplicity, and Road Vultures pulled their set of originals and punk-era covers off as well as could be expected in an empty room. Ex-Dead Boy Cheetah Chrome is featured on their Circumstantial Records debut, and reportedly plays at some gigs…but not this one.

***

ROAD VULTURES
Fire It Up (Circumstantial) The Road Vultures are a Brooklyn-based band that plays loud, glammy, amusingly offensive songs about life's simple pleasures (i.e.: sex, drugs and rock and roll—at least one song about each). Former Dead Boy Cheetah Chrome plays guitar on three tracks, including a cover of Johnny Thunders' "Chatterbox", which makes sense, as The Dead Boys, Thunders and the New York Dolls are their most obvious influences (the record is dedicated to the late Stiv Bators, Thunders and Jerry Nolan). Yeah, it's tasteless, and helplessly retro, but it's unpretentious enough to offer some entertainment if you like the bands they're borrowing from. [CD]
(*12 Seventh Avenue, Brooklyn, NY 11217*)
—*Andrew Johnston*

***

FRIDAY, Feb. 19: Don't stay home tonight— Keith Richards, with Soul Asylum at The Beacon Theatre, White Zombie and Monster Magnet at Industry Rocks, Arcade (w/ Steve Pearcy of Ratt, and Fred Coury of Cinderella) at Sparks, Road Vultures at Atlantis.

HEY AUNT HELEN ! - 117

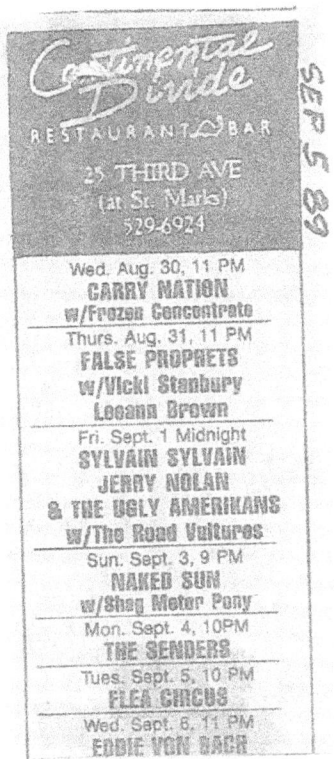

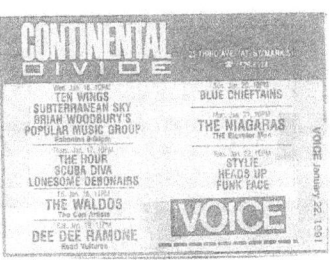

118 - KEVIN K

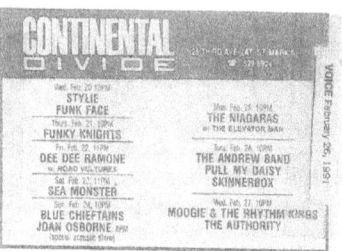

HEY AUNT HELEN ! - 119

Alan's drawing of Johnny Thunders apartment

120 - **KEVIN K**

Kevin .. Cheetah Chrome .. Alan 1991

Alan's Dope Bag Collection NYC

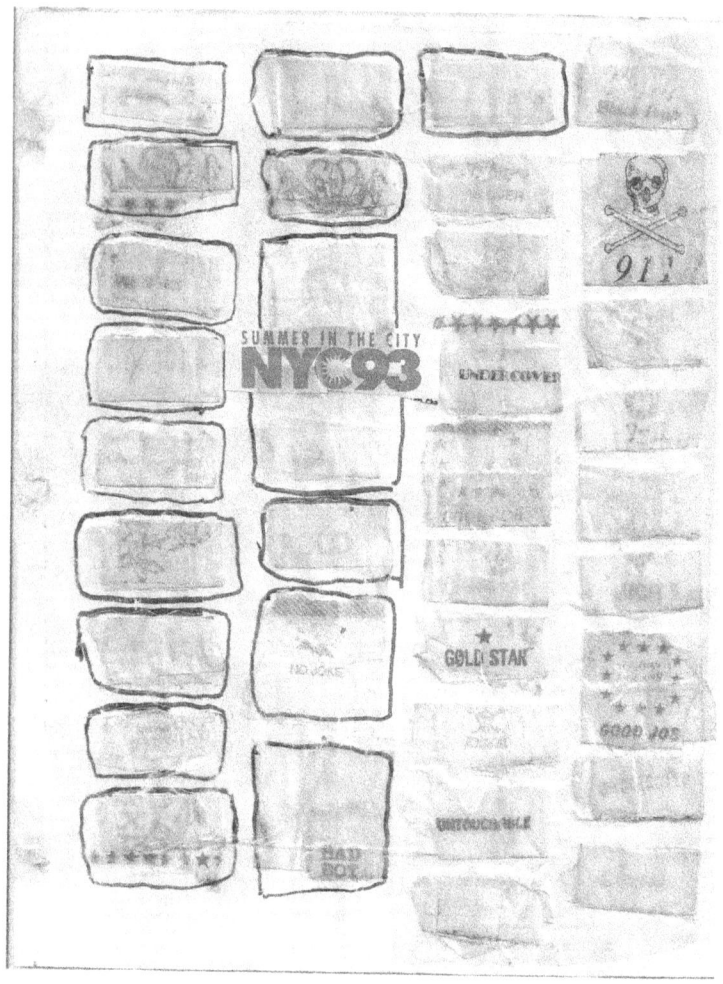

From Richard Hell ..
To Alan K ..Take the Best care of Yourself..
July 12 1996 ..
Alan K .. Died Nov 11 1996

HEY AUNT HELEN ! - 125

This is Alan's hand-drawn comic strip called 'STIV' – The Flying Rat Over the Lower East Side.

KEVIN K

BY: ALAN K

1. STIV SAYS:

"Gee I'm real happy to get these wings cause now I can eat more and get fatter and now be able to move as fast as little Twirly-Bird Camebriene

Weeeeeeee

I can't wait to run into my new neighbor Iggy Pop!!

3. Iggy casually waves to Stiv the flying rat, enjoying a grandiose, subliminal but nevertheless convuluted day in the pleasant East Village.

4. LOOKING IN ON ONE OF IGGYS WINDOWS, STIV FIGURES IGGY MUST BE WORKING ON NEW SONGS.. STIV ALSO NOTES THE LEFT HANDED GUITAR IGGY PLAYS

Jerry Nolan on my drums, NYC, 1989

| 17 |

ST. MARKS RECORD STORE GOODBYE

The closing of Sounds ended the final chapter of my life in New York City. I would visit the store every time I went back to New York. Brian, the owner, came out to my last couple of shows in 2014. We always had fun. Many drinks and talk about the old days. Brian told me he should have closed the store in the 1990's because business started to fall. For some reason, he continued on. I always wanted the Thunders poster that was up on the wall at the back of the store. It was a purple and white advertisement for a Johnny Thunders show at Irving Plaza. Super cool and old. It had water marks from the air conditioner that was hanging from the ceiling and was probably from 1976.

Brian showed me the backroom. He had the original *Born To Lose* poster on the wall. He said that when he permanently closed the store, he would give them to me. This never happened. Brian died in 2017. I think his health was not good. He always had a cigarette in his hand. Brian said he was going to have a plaque put in the sidewalk in front with all our names on it with the Sounds logo. I thought that was a fantastic idea. Sad that it never happened. The store closed very fast with no advertising at all. Just some Sounds paper bags taped to the staircase saying, 'closing sale.' Even today, I have dreams that I'm still working there. So weird.

Joe the store manager, and Tally, both also died a few years ago. Really good friends of mine. I remember working at Sounds in 1984, and Carol from CBGB called me and told me a special show was going on. This was December 9, 1984. A band named Gary and the Boners was playing. Yup, it was The Replacements. The club was packed, and Paul Westerberg was sitting on the stairs by the pool table. I said, 'Hi' and Paul said, 'Hi' and that was it. He didn't seem too happy.

Also, during the day Paul and Tommy came into Sounds. Binky said to me, 'Kevin, see those two guys at the back of the store looking at records. It's the Replacement guys.' They looked like two drunk kids. In the song *Alex Chilton*, there is the lyric, 'Checking my tracks on St Marks Place.' Maybe Paul wrote that after visiting Sounds. That night at CBGB, when they started to play, it was all covers. Sloppy, no endings to the songs. Still, it was great. I think Bob Stinson was wearing a nurse's outfit.

Another Sounds story. This was probably 1985. Sounds always had many A&R people coming in selling their promos of the latest releases on their labels, like Sire, Capitol, Warner Bros. etc. We had the new record from The Alarm on sale for $3.99. Many copies of it on the front rack. I get a call from a label guy telling me Mike Peters from The Alarm is on his way to visit the store. What? I immediately took all the $3.99 Alarm records off the rack and put them behind the counter, then took a few 'non promo' records and put them on the rack at $6.99. Within five minutes the door opens and its Mike Peters. He says, 'Hey thanks for having The Alarm record on the front rack.' HA, as I push the $3.99 Alarm records with my foot behind the counter.

We, as Lone Cowboys, used to play at Folk City in 1983. I remember The Replacements first show was at this club. I might have been at this show too, yet it's hard to remember all the shows I saw that year.

In 2018, I played a show at Sidewalk Café on Ave A. Walking back to the 13th Street apartment, Ritchie M. and I went past the new Coney Island Baby Bar. I look inside and there is Jesse Malin and a few other people sitting at the bar. We go in and Jesse says, 'Hey man, I know you!' Great time. We talked for an hour about the old days. I told Jesse he is the king of New York. He laughed at that. That's the thing that I miss most in my life. Walking down the street and seeing someone you haven't seen in years, but it feels like it was yesterday.

| 18 |

BYE BYE MOM

In 2014, Florence was diagnosed with dementia. Her doctor sent us to see many other doctors, to do test after test. In fact, I saw how a 'Pill Doctor' works. I don't remember his name. The office was in St. Petersburg. He asked Florence many questions that I thought she would never have an answer for. 'Where did you work when you lived in Buffalo?' Florence says, 'Upson Factory. In the mail department. Also, I worked for Harry Jacobs (former Buffalo Bills player) as a secretary.' Wow! She remembered life forty years ago. Then he asked her the name of the President. 'Kennedy', she replied. She didn't know current life. The doctor prescribed five different medications. It made her a zombie. She also had eye problems. The eye drops for a tiny little bottle were $500 that were not covered by insurance. Florence was feeling like a guinea pig. A test animal. She would never want to eat when we ate. Then at 10:00 PM, she would say, 'Let's eat dinner.'

Washing became a problem. She didn't want to take a bath. So I thought, *how can I make this fun?* I bought a nice healthy bubble bath, put a very comfortable rug in the tub, plus a bathrobe. She loved it. She would ask me every day, 'When can I take a bath?' Now, no doctors gave me any information about solving these small problems. It was always, 'Florence needs to be in a nursing home for proper care.' About one week later, I found her bathrobe in the garbage. She told me, 'I hate that robe.'

I came home after being on tour for three weeks. Alvin says, 'There was an incident.' Alvin came home from shopping and Florence was not in the house. He looked everywhere. He called the Pinellas Park Police. They finally found her after a thirty minute search. She was sitting in the bushes of the neighbor's yard covered in dirt.

Alvin asks her, 'Why were you sitting in the bushes?' Florence says, 'That wasn't me.' At night sometimes, Alvin wouldn't see her sleeping in her bed. He would find her standing in their closet. She would say, 'That's not my bed.' I knew it was over because at dinner time we always listened to Frank Sinatra. Florence would sit in front of the CD player and sing. So, I did a test. We're trying to have dinner with her. I put on Frank, and Florence gets up, walks right past the CD player into her bedroom. Now, I know it's over. I put locks on all the doors so Florence wouldn't walk out the door at night.

About three months later she bumps her head on the

bathroom wall. There is a little blood. I made the biggest mistake by taking her to hospital emergency. She was in there for two days. Test after test. Nothing wrong. The bills are $5,000. Guinea pig. Now they tell me she needs to go spend time in recovery at Gracewood Nursing Home.

We drop her off. Disgusting. Smells like shit. Old people everywhere. I saw the Grim Reaper in one room. Or maybe it was Marilyn Manson. Extremely grotesque.

Florence is there for nine weeks. Everyday Gracewood would call for us to bring in our bank statements. I asked a lot of questions about her walking, exercising, etc. No answers. Never met her doctor. The following week Alvin says, 'We are getting her out of there today!'

We march in through the doors. Alvin says, 'I'm here to pick up my wife and take her home. Fuck you if you think you can stop me.'

They won't even let us use a wheelchair. We carry her out the front door. They call the police. Florida law says you can't do this unless the treating doctor writes a note. They were charging our insurance company $6,500 A WEEK! Guinea pig.

The next day a social worker comes by to check on Florence. She sees Florence playing with JJ and LuLu, the cats. She says, 'OK. This is good.'

Two weeks later she is feeling sick again. She is now in a different nursing home in Largo. The next say they call me and say, 'Please go to St. Petersburg Emergency Hospital. Your mother is there.' Alvin and I speed over there. I get a $125 ticket for driving too fast.

We get there and she is in bed. She had fallen at the nursing home, where you are meant to be safe from this happening, and had broken her shoulder. She is screaming and crying. They medicate her. The doctor tells us she now has to go back to the nursing home for recovery. Alvin and I carry her to the car because if the hospital transported her back it would cost $750 and it is not covered by my insurance. Guinea pig.

We get her in the front seat. I'm driving and Florence says, 'I'm not going back there. I'm done.' I say, 'Look, go there for a week, we will come back and pick you up.' She says, 'No.' When we get to the nursing home no one says anything to Alvin and me about what happened. They put her in a wheelchair and take her inside. Alvin and I are just standing there. We get in the car and drive home. We hear no information from anyone. Two days later at 4:00 AM there is a loud knocking on our door. It's the Pinellas Park Police. The officer says, 'Your mother, Florence died. Her heart stopped last night.'

That was it. Never heard from her doctor about what happened. I'm still angry. I feel I let her down. Florence became a part of the Florida medical system. When that happens, you lose all control. Her insurance had no coverage in home care. She had to be in a nursing home. I'm the guinea pig. I don't think our government will ever find a cure for dementia. Why? There are billions of dollars made in treatments and drugs. The entire health care system in America is run on that. What would they replace it with to make money? We can send a guy to the Moon to hit a golf ball, but we can't stop cancer? Alvin and I talked about Florence for a week, and since then, nothing. It's the U.S. Army training he has ingrained in his mind. Someone dies, you leave them and move on.

About two weeks after her death, the funeral home called me and said, 'Kevin, your mom is ready for pick up.' If I didn't pick them up in one week, they take the remains by boat out to sea and unload them. So, I have her cremated remains in a little box on the front seat. I talked to her the entire drive back. Just like I did with Alan.

When I get to our house, I put her little box in a bigger box because we were in the middle of moving. Ten minutes later I hear a lot of scratching. I look and see the cats LuLu and JJ scratching to get into the box. Freaks me out to think about it. I never told Alvin nothing.

Also, last year I got a call from the St. Petersburg newspaper asking about Gracewood. I tell them, 'It's disgusting. Why is it even open?' The reporter says, 'Yes, we know. The paper is doing a story about the bad treatment of patients there.' A 90 year-old was left in the afternoon sun and died in his wheelchair. He baked to death. A Gracewood employee forgot to check on him. Baked guinea pig. Disgust.

| 19 |

JJ

It's a rain grey day today. A good setting for this story. In my first book, I talked about Joey the cat. He was with me for twelve years. A great cat. JJ was the kind of cat a person only has once in a lifetime. I had him for seven years. He made himself available twenty-four hours a day. Always ready for fun. JJ did a fantastic job in covering up his poops. He would work on that for five minutes, even when LuLu would poop, JJ would go in the box and cover her poop up too!

He loved watching the birds and squirrels and being in the garage with me as I was creating my muddy music. When we moved to Buffalo, JJ liked it. I still remember when we arrived in Cheektowaga on April 15 and it was snowing. I couldn't find the cats in the house! Then I found JJ and LuLu sitting on a box looking out the window watching the snow. They had that look on their faces of, 'What the fuck?'

My upstairs bedroom was always cold and that's where JJ always was. He loved it. I think he was from up north. Both cats also had fun in the basement, running around the Jerry Nolan drums.

They did well flying to Buffalo and then back to Florida. The house we moved back into in Florida had a backyard surrounded by a fence so JJ could go and have a good time.

He was never sick, and then in May of 2017 he would throw up. It was like *The Exorcist* movie. The puke would fly two feet out of him. Afterwards, he would sit there and drink water and go outside.

I took him to the doctor after about a month of him throwing up every day. They did blood tests which were OK, but when they did his x-rays, they found he had a small tumor in his stomach. The vet told me I could put him to sleep, which is what the average person would have done, or I could give him special treatments. I chose that because he was still healthy and not laying around. He was very active. It began. I had to feed him with a syringe with a steroid in it and wet food. He did not like this. After about three weeks, he was great. No problems. They found that the steroids had reduced the size of the tumor, but now he was getting diabetes. I think he covered up the fact that he was sick. He would still go outside and run around and chase lizards. Five months later, he began to throw up again, but only once a week.

We sold our house fast but had nowhere to live. We could not find a house to rent. I was going nuts trying to take care of Alvin, JJ and then the hurricane! I would come home and just lay down on the floor of my room spaced out. JJ knew something was up with me. He would come into the room and lay next to me and put his head on my head and just stare at me. It came down to three days. We had to be out of the house in three days. The guy calls and says he has a house for us to rent in downtown St. Petersburg. We go to see it. It is great and has a long hallway where JJ could run down super fast.

Alvin and I came home. We were happy and at peace. JJ jumps on my lap. I give him a twenty minute back rub. He eats a whole can of food. I go to sleep, the best I have felt in three weeks. At 6:00 AM I hear the sound of loud cat cries. There is JJ next to my bed and he is on his side. His heart is going a hundred miles an hour. I pick him up and put him outside, thinking maybe he will just run away. I call the doctor, she says to bring him in right now. I go outside. He hasn't moved. I get him in the car. At the vets they freak out and take him. He is having a heart attack. I leave and go home. About an hour later they call to tell me the tumor exploded and his lungs are filled with fluid. He is done. Well, I cried for three days. In fact I am almost crying now, but that just tells you how much that cat meant to me. Goodbye JJ.

The doctor told me I did an amazing job with his care. JJ had gained weight, and the vet couldn't believe how good he looked. They said almost no one would go through what I did. I had added at least eight months to his life.

So, in looking back, I think JJ was really sick, but he was hiding it from me. He knew what I was going through. He saw I was happy and feeling good. He did his job and checked out.

The power of animals is amazing to me. It is very spiritual. I received a few condolence cards for JJ. He was liked by everybody. I waited a few months before looking for a new cat. Then the ASPCA (American Society for the Prevention of Cruelty to Animals) called to tell me to come see this cool guy they had. This was the same ASPCA where JJ came from.

I first looked at about ten cats, yet none of them did anything for me. And then, there he is! JERRY. Four years old, and the same age as JJ was when we got him. Again, I have a new best friend. I can picture him living with me in an apartment on the Lower East Side someday.

Just now, as I am finishing this story, one of my singles fell off the shelf above me and hit me in the head. The single that fell was *Fire It Up* with the cat on the front! It's the spirit of JJ telling me it's OK.

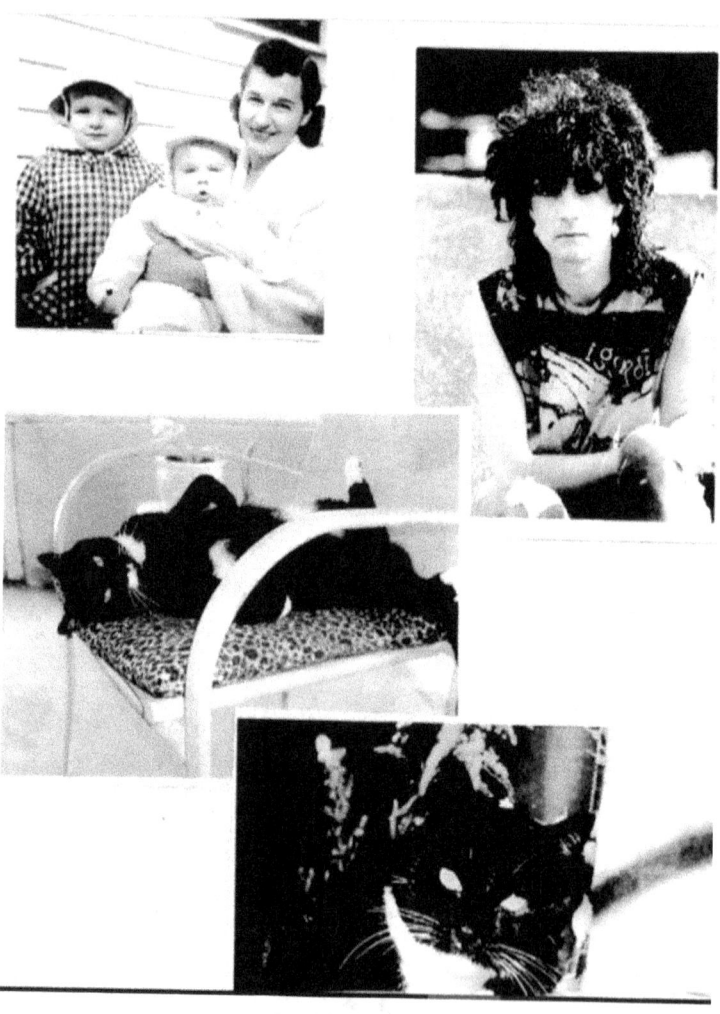

Dee Dee

Jerry and his banana

| 20 |

A POEM FOR LULU

I noticed LuLu having a hard time breathing. She would lay on her side all the time. She looked very uncomfortable. This went on for about three days. My first thought was that maybe Alvin had fallen on her because she would sleep in his bed right next to him. Maybe injured her back? So I put her in the car and went to the cat doctor down the street.

The doctor said she seemed to be really struggling taking in air. They do some x-rays while I wait outside. This took an hour. I'm freaking out. Finally, they call me in. 'Sorry Kevin, but on the x-rays you can see her lungs are filled from a small tumor that is leaking. She should be put to sleep.' I almost passed out. I had to grab on to the chair. How is this possible? The doctor tells me there is a place in Clearwater that specializes in a procedure that drains the fluid out of lungs. This could be very expensive.

I found LuLu about twelve years ago. She was a little tiny lost girl. I saw her at night outside crying in a big rainstorm. I left the door open with some food. In the morning, the food was gone but no cat around. That night, again the same thing. She was outside looking at me, and when I opened the door she ran away. Didn't see her for two days.

Again, I left the door open with some food. In the morning when I checked again, there she was sleeping on the chair. I went to visit her and she didn't move. A lot of her hair was missing. Maybe from a cat fight? After that, she was happy and stayed inside.

I took her to the vet to see if she was sick or had a disease. They did blood work and she checked out clean. What a super cat she turned into. LuLu became my mother's cat. Always sleeping in her bed. Florence would sit with her as she ate and would make sure she finished all her food. Then she would comb her. LuLu was her best friend. LuLu was tough. Probably from being outside and lost. Joey would sometimes fight with her, but she never backed down.

About five years later she needed to have many teeth pulled out because they were hurting her. I dropped her off at the dentist in the morning. About six hours later, I picked her up and brought her home. She had a hard time walking but was fine the next day.

When Joey died, she knew something was bad. After a few months, my mother found JJ's picture in the paper, up for adoption. So, we brought him home and LuLu was totally cool with him.

When my mother died, LuLu was very sad. This was so hard to get through. Alvin, LuLu, JJ and I all moved to Buffalo for eight months. The cats did well on the plane flights and were amazed by the snow outside the house. Good times. We moved back to Florida because the VA gave Alvin a loan for a house. Really good. We spent no money at all.

In 2017, LuLu had the rest of her teeth removed. Now she had no teeth. Still, it did not bother her at all. She loved whip cream after dinner.

JJ died later that year. So hard to deal with. Again, LuLu was by herself. I just had so much respect for LuLu. She used all her nine lives for sure. So, I had many drinks, put LuLu in the car and drove like a maniac to Clearwater. They told me they could drain the fluids from her lungs and she could be OK for a while, or it could refill.

I decide to go for it. Very expensive. LuLu sat in the window of the doctor's office looking outside, not fazed by anything, no crying, unbelievable. At 9:00 PM they call me to come pick her up, she is OK.

I bring her home and she could not even walk. The medication completely hurt her. I thought she was going to die that night. Jerry slept right next to her. In the morning, she wouldn't eat.

The next day LuLu couldn't breathe again. Again I drove like a crazy man to the vet's office. LuLu sat next to me in the car. No crying, no complaints. She gave me that look of 'let me go.' When I got there, they told me it was time to let her go. That was it. I said goodbye to LuLu.

This cat was so strong in her 14-year life. I can't believe what she went through, and she never made a fuss. I will never have another cat like this. She taught me to be strong every day. The power of animals is amazing. The BEST. Jerry would sleep in the bed with me but after LuLu left us, he wouldn't be on the bed. When I looked for him at night, he was sleeping on the chair where LuLu used to sleep every night. This drove me crazy sad. After a month, I couldn't take it anymore. Jerry needed a friend.

I went to the SPCA where I got Jerry. I saw many cats but none of them impressed me.

Then, there she is! I see this beautiful calico cat. Her name is Dee Dee, fantastic! She has the same personality of LuLu. Has a big bushy tail like her too and the same colors of brown and white. I play with her in her cage with about five other cats. As I'm leaving, she follows me right out the door into the hallway. The woman that takes care of the cats said, 'Wow, she really wants to go home with you.'

So now, I have Jerry and his girlfriend Dee Dee. She is a special little girl. The playing is so great, they are so happy together. Jerry is always washing her. He is a playboy now. Dee Dee bites me, just like LuLu, and she sits in the same spot as LuLu did when she eats.

But this really freaks me out. When I open the refrigerator door, Dee Dee comes running and sits right in front. I open the whipped cream container and put a little on her face. She loves it! This is the same thing that LuLu used to do! How can that be? It's amazing. These cats are the only thing that save me from going completely crazy. I have a new song called *Let Me Go LuLu* which I will record soon.

Bye Bye LuLu. Miss you!

Alvin and Kevin in 2015 in front of the house at 6357 Main Road. Everything still looks the same !

The Pendleton NY garage where it all started in 1974 - and the first Aunt Helen rehearsals in 1976

The back porch - where in 1968 I first heard Jumpin' Jack Flash while listening to the radio outside

| 21 |

KEVIN K DAYS

Alvin and I had to sign our mortgage papers in Buffalo at City Hall. We met our lawyer there and waited for about one hour for someone from the Bank of America. Finally, this hot looking girl shows up with a stack of papers.

Right from the start she had an attitude. Its page after page of fifty pages. While this happens, I have a conversation with our lawyer who is sitting across from us.

He says, 'So Kevin, what type of guitar do you have?' I say, 'Well, it's a fifty year old Gibson Melody Maker. Probably worth a lot of money.' The girl from Bank of America interrupts us and says, 'Well, you know Kevin, if you don't make your mortgage payments on time, Bank of America will own that guitar!' WHAT? You piece of crap, how dare you say that to me. I almost got up and walked out. The lawyer just shook his head. Afterwards, he said that was a terrible joke.

I tried to open a bank account with $300. I went to five different banks, and they turned me down. It wasn't even worth it for them to open with that small amount of money. Damn, I guess I should bury it in the backyard.

I'm at the airport going through security. My bag is being scanned. I am taken over to get hand frisked. It's a young guy. Seems OK, asks me what band I'm in. I tell him my name. He says, 'Oh, I know who you are.' Then, as I am picking up my bag, an older woman who is an officer with the TSA (Transportation Security Administration) stops me. We start talking, lots of questions. Where am I going? My name. After she's done, she says to me, 'You know I'm a cougar.' WHAT? I didn't know what to say to her. A cougar is an expression for an older person who acts like a younger person and wants sex. It probably would have been fun. She had a set of handcuffs on her belt. I was in a hurry. I had to use the toilet.

As I am boarding the plane a guy stops me and says, 'Hey, aren't you the singer from the Scorpions?' I say, 'No. I'm the singer from the Groundhogs.' I looked on the internet for photos of the singer from the Scorpions. He is fat and bald! I thought, *I still look like a combination of Johnny Depp and Justin Bieber.*

Now, I am checking out at the supermarket called Publix. Really nice-looking young girl at the register. We're talking, and she is packing my bag with toilet paper, Metamucil, Bengay back cream and Corona beer. Old people items. As I'm paying her, and after seeing my tattoos she says to me, 'Wow, you must have been the man in your day!'

I'm shopping at Target, a department store. I'm going out the door. I hear, 'Wait. Stop!' It's the security guard. He says to me, 'You know, you look just like Ozzy Osbourne.' It's better than someone saying I look like a young Richard Nixon. I think I need to stay home and order all my stuff on Amazon.

| 22 |

WHICH MASK ARE YOU ?

2020 is over. It took a lot of people away. It took many cities away, especially NYC. This was the center of entertainment, now it's a ghost town. It will come back, but with new leaders. Governor Cuomo was responsible for 16,000 old people dying in nursing homes.

When will clubs have 100 people in them, dancing, drinking and listening to live bands again? It might not happen until 2022.

Walter Lure left us, so did Sylvain Sylvain. It's unbelievable to me. Walter seemed to be doing really well, playing lots of shows and the new Waldos CD *Wacka Lacka Loom Bop A Loom Bam Boo* is great. I don't know who represents NYC music anymore. I guess no one.

Ricky Rat was here in St Pete last March to play a show at the Emerald Bar. It was really wild. Good fun. We also recorded the *Party Store* CD. We both knew everything was gonna stop. I didn't think it would last a whole year, probably longer.

I now smoke more and drink more. I think a lot of people are. What else is there to do? This is our World War III and we are losing. This mask thing can't be good for us, breathing in all the bad fumes that are supposed to be let out of our bodies.

I have been busy writing and recording demos, but now I am starting to miss touring and just playing live shows. I hate all this virtual or Zoom shows. I am not into that. I need a live audience or a girl in front of me with large breasts to give me inspiration.

I guess all this has taught me I had to develop more of my own independence. I have become an endangered species.

Three things for the rest of my life:

1. I don't want to be over reliant on other people.
2. I won't ever lose myself.
3. I will NEVER grow up.

| 23 |

DETROIT ROCK CITY 2022

So, I sold mine and Alvin's house in Florida. I had one open house and 300 people came to see it. I worked hard the last year painting and planting bushes and flowers. It looked great. When we bought it in January of 2020 the guy who lived there – Walter, did nothing to keep it up. He was a smoker inside for 30 years. It took me two months to wash the walls and ceiling. It was unbelievable to see the towels I used to wipe the walls, would be the color brown from tobacco. The day we moved in Walter was laying on the couch smoking. I yelled at him 'Get the fuck out of my house! You don't live here anymore.' He got up and walked out the door with two suitcases, that's it. He left everything…all the furniture, pots, pans, food and beer in the refrigerator - plus all his socks, cloths and underwear. It was crazy. I bought his plane flight to Philadelphia, where he was going to move in with his sister. I paid his car towing and gave him $1000 in cash. It was a good deal for him - and Alvin. Update: About three months later there's a knock at the door. It's Walter. He says, "I had a fight with my sister, I'm back, you want to sell the house back to me?" I shut the door. That same day I had junkers (guys who remove stuff) come by and took all the furniture and a 100-pound safe that was in the closet.

After months of clean-up the house was nice, probably the best one for Alvin to live in. It was a VA loan which was good because as a Veteran, Alvin paid nothing to move in - just the first mortgage payment of $1020. This was the fifth VA loan we used, so I feel good that at least we took full advantage of this offer from the VA. Alvin was not attached to anything, he told me if you want to fix this house up and sell it he was OK with that. We looked into moving to Michigan in 2018.

So now it's Sept 22, 2020, and my hero and best friend Alvin leaves me. The mortgage immediately goes to $1655 a month. I also lose all the VA benefits and have to pay $2500 to Probate Court because they don't accept Alvin's will from 1986. I thought about suicide many times, because I have nothing to live for, you know? What stopped me was Alvin. He would have been furious at me for doing something like that. When my mother died, he would say things like 'Move on, she's dead' - and they were married 62 years.

Well, I did one year and seven months unloading grocery trucks. I won't even make enough money to pay my bills for every month. Winn-Dixie grocery was my first job in twenty four years. I saw twenty people and five managers quit. The shoplifting at the store and the homeless in the parking lot was very dangerous - the police were at the store every week. We found a guy laying on the floor in the men's room overdosed on fentanyl. My last manager told me I was the best and hardest worker at the store, and I worked nine days in a row many times. I actually liked the job. It was so different for me. It got to the point I had no boss, I would sign in and do my job stacking shelves, customer service etc. In fact, the store did not close one day throughout the entire covid period. You could wear a mask if you wanted. I had covid and I was sick for five days with fever and body aches. I took at least fifty cold tablets, plus I drank a lot of water, did a lot of walking and it passed.

The days at the store would fly by. Plus, it took my mind off of losing Alvin. Florida's population has increased by 230,000 people in one year. And that's the problem! The traffic and noise are insane. The house prices have increased by amounts that a lot of old people can't afford anymore. I tried very hard to stay in the house and not move. It was impossible. The taxes went to $2660 and a new roof was needed ($18,500 for that).

Plus, what was difficult for me was coming home from work or rehearsal and Alvin's not there. Or that's Alvin's chair or there's the squirrel that Alvin used to feed. I cried a lot. It wasn't good for me mentally. I wrote about 40 new songs and worked on this book so that helped me.

July 5th, 2022. Jerry and Dee Dee board their van ride of twenty-one hours to Michigan. I'm not too happy about that. My realtor comes to pick me up and take me to Tampa airport. I feed the birds and squirrels for the last time. I took care of at least thirty of them - they will miss me and the cats. In the car, I look at the house for the last time and wave to the banana tree I planted in the front yard for Alvin. It's surrealistic.

Alvin's banana tree

I picked Michigan because house prices are lower, and I have friends there. I am tired of dealing with heat and humidity and hurricanes. Plus, Florida was always the state where Alan and I would vacation and relax with our parents. They are all gone now. It's weird to have windows open in July. Jerry and Dee Dee are amazed by it. The cats did great on their van ride. Jerry told me it was fun to look out the window at Kentucky. My house is red brick, built solid in 1952. There is a nice backyard and finished basement. Looks like the Kenmore/Snyder area of Buffalo. Well I don't know if I'm happy or still confused by everything that has happened to me in the last two years. In a way, I feel I'm damaged now.

Plus, I now have no roots anywhere. NYC is over for me, Florida is over too. With my family all gone it's difficult to find where I belong now. I guess the answer is anywhere I want. Maybe that's a good thing .

I look at everything as one year. I will see how I feel or how my music is doing or how Jerry and Dee Dee are doing. Maybe I move again? Probably, my next move would be to Lockport/Pendleton where my life first began. Maybe I could search the woods in front of the Pendleton Main Road house and look for the hockey pucks I shot there 45 years ago

| 24 |

ALVIN – MY ROCK 'N' ROLL DAD

So I knew it could happen at any time, but still it's hard to deal with. Alvin was the Best Dad – and my best friend.

I loved his tenacity – he had that military fight in him until the end.

If he didn't like you or the situation he was in, he would tell you straight up. I used this when I got the chance to yell at one of the main doctors at Bay Pines. The guy was shocked what I told him. I'm sure Alvin was laughing wherever he is.

Alvin should have been home with me, not in the hospital for almost five days. They didn't let me see him or talk to him because of the virus, even though he didn't have it. He gave up, probably didn't think I was coming to get him.

I would always come see him the next day when he was in emergency and tell him, 'Remain calm, listen to what the doctors say, I will come get you to take you home. We can drink a beer and watch baseball.' Alvin would smile and say, 'OK!'

Bay Pines Hospital admitted they made mistakes. God damn horrible. My last family member is now buried in Sarasota, two hours away from me.

Alvin was my biggest cheerleader. He saw me play outside last year at a record store. He loved Lemmy from Motorhead's voice and also the Probot CD. Alvin thought Johnny Thunders and Iggy Pop were just amazing performers. Not only the music but how they interacted with their audiences.

I got Alvin and Florence on the guest list for an Iggy Pop show here in St. Petersburg in 1998. Alvin got backstage and met Iggy. He told me he had to wait fifteen minutes in a hallway, and he could see Iggy walking back and forth in the dressing room trying to calm down. Alvin had on his Stooges t-shirt. Iggy saw it and said, 'Hey I like that shirt!' They took a photo together, but I never got a copy of it.

As recently as August 2020, I came home from rehearsal and Alvin was sitting at the table and first thing he said to me was, 'How was the practice? Did you play good?' This is from a 95-year-old guy. Now I come home and he's not there. Very sad for me. I miss him very much.

So I have decided to sell my house. Everything is off the walls except Alvin's Army photo and story from the *The Buffalo News*, and his medals.

I had over 340 people come to see the house in one day. I set a record for house showings in one day. Everybody who came to see the house all looked at the wall and read Alvin's story – thanking him for his service to our country.

Alvin is here with me, helping to sell the house. I will do really well. Its Alvin's gift to me.

| 25 |

KEVIN K DISCOGRAPHY (1978-2022)

AUNT HELEN, 1978: *Big Money b/w Rebecca* [7" single]
THE TOYS, 1980: *Livin' Fast b/w I'm Tellin' You Now* [7" single]
NEW TOYS, 1982: *Say It* [LP]
LONE COWBOYS, 1985: *You Light Up My Life b/w Skulls Have Eyes* [7" single]
LONE COWBOYS, 1985: *Streets Of Poison* [Cassette]
LONE COWBOYS, 1986: *Voodoo Dolls and Cadillac Fins* [LP]
ROAD VULTURES, 1993: *Fire It Up* [CD, Cassette]
ROAD VULTURES, 1994: *Skulls Have Eyes b/w You Light Up My Life* [7" single]
ROAD VULTURES, 1995: *Ride* [CD]
KEVIN K BAND, 1995: *Night Life* [CD]
KEVIN K BAND, 1996: *Never Enough* [Cassette]
KEVIN K BAND, 1996: *Party Down* [CD]
KEVIN K BAND, 1997: *Rule the Heart* [CD]
FREDDY LYNXX & THE CORNER GANG (KEVIN K BAND), 1998: Street Values b/w Have Faith [7" single]
KEVIN K AND THE ITALIAN ICES, 1998: Deadboy Runnin' Scared b/w Saint of the Gutter [7" single]
FREDDY LYNXX & THE CORNER GANG (KEVIN K BAND), 1998. "Fire It Up" / "Those Deep Blue Eyes" [7" single]

KEVIN K & THE GOLDEN ARMS, 1998: *Steppin Stone b/w Melody* [7" single]

KEVIN K BAND, 1999: Midnight Dragon / When I Knew You / Fire It Up [7" single EP]

FREDDY LYNXX & THE CORNER GANG (KEVIN K BAND), 1999: *Have Faith / Too Many Hearts* [7" single]

FREDDY LYNXX & THE CORNER GANG (KEVIN K BAND), 1999: *Bloodied Up* [CD]

KEVIN K, 1999: *Story of My Life* [CD]

KEVIN K BAND, 2000: *Oriental Nights: Live in Japan* [CD]

KEVIN K, 2000: *Magic Touch* [CD]

KEVIN K & SOUR JAZZ, 2001: *Arbeit Macht Frei – Live at Continental Divide* [CD]

KEVIN K, 2001: *13th Street* [CD]

KEVIN K, 2002: *From The Delta to the Bowery* [CD}

KEVIN K, 2002: *Sealed Works* [CD]

KEVIN K, 2002: *Better Class of Slut / How I Feel / New York City / Jennifer Love* [7" Single EP]

ROAD VULTURES, 2002: *Just Say Yes* [CD]

KEVIN K & THE REAL KOOL KATS, 2003: *Kiss of Death* [CD, LP]

KEVIN K & THE REAL KOOL KATS / NEUROTIC SWINGERS, 2003: (7" split single)

THE DISCIPLES, 2003: *Disciples* [CD]

KEVIN K & THE REAL KOOL KATS, 2004: *Addiction* [CD, Cassette]

KEVIN K, 2004: *New York, New York: Best of Collection* [CD, Cassette]

FREDDY LYNXX & THE CORNER GANG (KEVIN K BAND), 2004: *Full Cover* [CD]

KEVIN K & THE REAL KOOL KATS, 2005: *Perfect Sin* [CD]

KEVIN K & THE REAL KOOL KATS / SONIC ANGELS, 2005: (7" split single)

KEVIN K, 2005: *Mr. Bones* [CD]

KEVIN K, 2006: *Rockin' Roll Dynamite* [CD]

KEVIN K, 2006: *Polish Blood – Best of Collection* [CD]

NEW TOYS, 2006: *Better Late Than Never* [LP]

KEVIN K, 2007: *Hollywood* [CD]

KEVIN K AND THE HOLLYWOOD STARS, 2008: *Cool Ways* [CD]

KEVIN K AND THE ST. PETE ALLSTARS, 2009: *Palm Trees and Humidity* [CD]

KEVIN K, 2009: *How To Become A Successful Loser: Retrospective* [CD]

KEVIN K, 2009: *Deutschland* [CD]

KEVIN K & TEXAS TERRI, 2010: *Firestorm* [CD, LP]

KEVIN K, 2010: *Kool Kat Kollection* [2 x LP]

KEVIN K, 2011: *Joey and Me* [CD]

LESTER AND THE LANDSLIDE LADIES / KEVIN K, 2011: *Frantic Tales For The Fast Living* [split CD]

KEVIN K, 2012: *Tramp Stamp* [CD]

NEW TOYS, 2012: *Made In Buffalo* [CD]

KEVIN K AND THE KOOL KATS, 2013: *Allies* [CD, LP]

KEVIN K, 2014: *Hurt You* [CD]

KEVIN K, 2015: *Buffalo* [CD]

KEVIN K, 2016: *Manhattan Project* [CD]

KEVIN K, 2017: *End of Complications* [CD]

KEVIN K, 2017: *The CBGB Years* [CD]

KEVIN K AND THE KRAZY KATS, 2018: *Too Much Too Sun* [CD]

KEVIN K AND THE KRAZY KATS, 2018: Just Say Yes b/w Dry Drunk [7" single]

KEVIN K AND RICKY RAT, 2020: *Party Store* [CD]

KEVIN K AND RICKY RAT, 2021: *Identity Crisis b/w Song For LuLu* [7" single]

AUNT HELEN / THE TOYS / LONE COWBOYS, 2022: *Hey Aunt Helen!* [CD]

KEVIN K, 2022: *Cadallac Man* [CD]

HEY AUNT HELEN! CD (Vicious Kitten Records)
1. Aunt Helen – Big Money (1978)
2. Aunt Helen – Rebecca (1978)
3. Aunt Helen – Family Jewels (1978)
4. Aunt Helen – House Guests (1978)
5. Aunt Helen – Too Much Make Up (1978)
6. Aunt Helen – Teenage Pig (1978)
7. The Toys – Livin' Fast (1980)
8. The Toys – I'm Telling You Now (1980)
9. The Toys – Running Away (1980)
10. The Toys – Instant Suicide (1980)
11. The Toys – Don't Know Why (1980)
12. The Toys – Should Have Known Better (1980)
13. Lone Cowboys – Lost Weekend (1983)
14. Lone Cowboys – Yellow Flower (1983)

My hero and best friend

www.ingramcontent.com/pod-product-compliance
Lightning Source LLC
Chambersburg PA
CBHW050312010526
44107CB00055B/2202